To my grandparents, John and Sue Howes,

who taught me the importance of hard work,

faith, education and country.

PRAISE FOR COMBAT TO COLLEGE

"Going forward, I'm handing this to every one of my soldiers who are starting college, it takes powerful combat and military lessons and applies them in a straightforward way. Every single veteran I know struggles adjusting to college life, here is the solution"
Samuel Brooks, Army Ranger, Bronze Star, Purple Heart Recipient

"Throughout my 22-year military career, I've watched Reservists and Guard personnel stumble their way through school with varying results. It can be hard to relate to your peers and find your place in the classroom as a veteran, this helps you create your place. Veterans should embrace their status in the classroom, not hide from it to fit in. It's inspiring and hard-hitting and deserves a lot of attention from the military community"
Master Sergeant (Retired) Dan Collelo, Army National Guard

"Military families have a unique set of circumstances that other students just don't have to deal with. I'd recommend this book for spouses, children and all military families to deal with the challenge's college brings to veterans. As a current college student, I loved reading this"
Shannon Duarte, Gold Star Wife

"This is well worth the time to everyone interested in college. This will especially benefit student athletes who will gain a lot from embracing a winning military mindset. I didn't put it down, combat veterans of this great country have a lot to teach us"

Pat Angerer, Former NFL Linebacker, Iowa Hawkeye

"As a former student veteran myself and someone who has worked for years to help student veterans through the VFW, I know first-hand what veterans contend with in classrooms. The dropout rates for veterans are shockingly high, this is the practical book that will show veterans the right path"

Dave Rogers, Veterans of Foreign Wars Commander, Army Veteran

"It's painfully honest but entertaining, a window into the struggles student veterans face including alcoholism, PTSD and isolationism. Now they don't have to face them alone but instead with this in hand. An extremely useful read for every military affiliated student"

Kevin Porter, Author of *Joining the Military: Everything you need to know your Recruiter won't tell you*

"I was absorbed for every chapter of this book. This book is necessary, for all veterans and anyone who wants to maximize their success in education. You can count on this book to change you for the better, like a trusted friend giving you advice"

Sgt Nathan MacDougall, Iraq/Afghanistan Veteran

"Nobody teaches you how to transition from the extremely struc-tured nature of the military into the weird world of college. Most veterans transition out of the military straight into college and it proves to be too much of a burden in many cases. Leading to high dropout rates, depression and even suicide. To be clear, this book will benefit every single person that reads it, increasing their odds of success and graduation. I learned a lot"

Ron Hurtado, Army Veteran, Founder of Airborne Triathlon Team

"Reading this makes you realize how few people rise to their true potential. Support systems are crucial to being successful during college and in life for veterans. This provides enormous value to demonstrate how military experience can help, not hinder your academic goals. The lessons are easy to implement and just make sense"

Jaime Aparicio, Navy Veteran, Student Veterans of America President, Team Rubicon

"I was wounded by a rocket attack in Afghanistan, I know first-hand the problems veterans juggle while trying to earn a degree. Dealing with PTSD, the VA, family, and transitioning out of the military feels impossible at times. The veterans who dropped out or thought they couldn't do it should pick up this book and go for it. I'm going back."

Captain Brien "Sandman" Durkee, Purple Heart Recipient

COMBAT TO COLLEGE

APPLYING THE
MILITARY MENTALITY TO THE CLASSROOM:
HOW TO SUCCEED AS A STUDENT VETERAN

JOHN H DAVIS

ISBN: 978-0-578-66338-8

CONTENTS

MISSION BRIEF

"In preparing for battle I have always found that plans are useless, but planning is indispensable."

Dwight D. Eisenhower

I went back to college at thirty. Prior to this, I had essentially flunked out of two community colleges before spending eight years in the military. My first week of classes, I told a fellow student to "shut the hell up, I was killing people in Afghanistan when you were eight years old." He certainly shut up, after being yelled at in a private college classroom by some bearded maniac covered in tattoos with a grunt-style shirt on. In the moment, I found a certain short-lived satisfaction in my proclamation and smugness in his submissive reaction. I thought I had put him in his place by asserting my military experience and dominance.

Looking back, I looked like a moron, embarrassing myself and, just as important, embarrassing my fellow veterans and

1

the military. I don't even recall the inconsequential point I was making at the time.

My second week didn't get any better. I get significant ringing in my ears after being blown up a few times in Afghanistan. A few times a week, I lose my hearing for a short time. Of course, this happens when the professor wants to ask me questions and I'm just looking at him pointing at my ear. He responds by trying to talk louder and more animatedly. The first time it happened, I yelled at him, "I can't fucking hear you, man, stop talking to me!"

Within my first week, I recognized the painful truth that there was no way I could endure years of acting like this, especially at the private school I was attending. I clearly had issues. I wouldn't be able to survive it, no way would I make it to my goal of graduation unless I adjusted my approach. I was going to have to figure some shit out, get mature quick, and reinvent myself. I'd have to somehow go from the guy who formerly perceived himself as a badass soldier to a studious college student; that is, if I wanted to find some measure of success. I reflected on how to transfer the hard-won skills I had gained in the military to my new college environment. I am, and always will be, a soldier. I knew how to work hard, be on time, and hold myself to a high standard. My time in the military had given me real-world experience. I knew how to be a member of a winning team, and I was willing to pay any price to be successful. I had these advantages over the other students, but I also had genuine disadvantages. I was used to the rigid, structured life of the military. Now, I was in an environment that I knew nothing about and was not qualified or trained for. I wasn't prepared. I had PTSD from Afghanistan and anxiety about my upcoming college mission. As a combat veteran I felt out of place in libraries, Starbucks, and on a college campus. I was more at home deployed in the Middle East or on a firing range than at school. I was focused solely on my disadvantages rather than the edge that my military experiences could provide me in my crusade for a college degree.

College is a different kind of challenge, and I had serious doubts about myself and my academic abilities. I realized I was scared—more scared than I had been of getting shot at in Afghanistan. It was terrifying to think about sitting in a college class. I felt way out of my element and too dumb to succeed at this brand-new chapter of my life. I had serious doubts about whether I belonged in college. Not having been enrolled in formal education in years, I had the illusion that students at universities and colleges were just smarter people than me. I never viewed myself as book smart. When I'd last attempted the whole college experience ten years earlier, I'd failed miserably and ended up enlisting in the Army.

My third go-around in college came after eight years in the military and multiple combat deployments. If college didn't work out this time, I would be fucked. I had no skills outside of combat-related tasks and no plan for my life if I couldn't cut it in school. I had the good fortune of attending a military-friendly school where I was able to participate in a work-study program through the Veteran's Administration. My role was to assist other veterans by ensuring they received their earned college benefits and to mentor them along the path to graduation. The program exists because the VA recognizes that a system of veterans helping veterans is effective at increasing graduation rates. I took my duties seriously. These duties included utilizing the leadership skills I gained in the Army to support other student veterans' academic and personal efforts, even during my struggles. In doing this, I learned common sense approaches to creating personal and academic growth in college for myself and others. Veterans need to utilize the skills that we all acquired during years of military service to thrive in modern classrooms. We all gained valuable life lessons, maturity, and grit in the military. I learned to not abandon my military mentality but to embrace, refine, and sharpen it for my new battlefield: the classroom.

College is a war for your future personal success and going

4

into battle you need all the resources and tools that you can muster. Like in real battles, give yourself every edge you possibly can, because your survival might depend on it. We all start somewhere; this is your new beginning. It's easy to be at the bottom of the mountain and want to reach the success that sits on top. The hard part is executing the grueling climb and navigating the obstacles in your path. Using the knowledge presented in this book, you can harness your military experiences and skills to create success in college. You'll learn skills like knowing not to scream "SHUT THE FUCK UP" at your teenage classmates—that is, unless they deserve it.

THIS IS YOUR NEW CONTRACT

*"Each and every day I get back up and move forward
with my fist clenched toward the battle."*

Jocko Willink

Oaths have long existed, and in a variety of forms. People have sworn oaths to various gods throughout history. People swear oaths to tell the truth in court, doctors take the Hippocratic Oath, new citizens take oaths of citizenship. You took an oath when you joined the military. Maybe you still remember it, maybe you don't, but it is a profound experience to swear into the military. I took the same oath. When I swore into the Army, I was making a promise to myself and my country, just like the men and women that came before me. It was a serious undertaking. The oath was the beginning of my military journey and an integral part of the transformation from civilian to soldier. Words have power. When you raised your right hand you were following a tradition that has historic roots tracing all the way back to the Revolutionary War. The original oath in 1775 read:

> I (NAME) have, this day, voluntarily enlisted myself, as a soldier, in the American continental army, for one year, unless sooner discharged: And I do bind myself to conform, in all instances, to such rules and regulations, as are, or shall be, established for the government of the said Army.

The words have been altered, but the spirit of the oath you took remains unchanged. You swore to do something, in a ceremony with people in a similar life position. You said the words shoulder to shoulder with other people who were stepping up to serve their country. Hopefully your loved ones were there, proud of you for your commitment and sacrifice for the greater good. You didn't want to let them or yourself down, and in a way you couldn't. The contract was somewhat legally binding. You couldn't exactly say "never mind" once you were in the military. Strolling off into the sunset wasn't an option; there were consequences.

In your new college environment, the consequences are different. There is no oath taken like the one above. This shouldn't be misconstrued to mean it is any less of an important commitment. The difference is who the commitment is to. Your oath to the military was to America, it was an oath of service and immensely important. Although your commitment to college is only to yourself and your future, your school contract has more in common with your military contract then you might think. While you were in the military, America got your blood, sweat, tears, and effort in return for your pay and benefits. Unless you are like me and lost the majority of that pay to ex-wives and booze. You give college your money, time, and effort, and they educate you in return. The education and the diploma are the reasons you are attending school. There are veterans who go to college and waste four years learning nothing but gain a diploma. Then there are veterans who genuinely learn a bit but never make it to graduation. There are veterans who start and never make it through a single semester, leaving frustrated and feeling like a failure. There were a few people I knew that didn't learn, didn't graduate, and ended up on a path to fucking nowhere. Don't be another bad veteran statistic. Be a success story. Commit yourself to both learning and graduating. Do all you can to put on that cap and gown to walk across the stage as a smarter and more capable person.

In this commitment to yourself, you are signing a new contract, both short term and long term, when you sign up for your classes. Think of your class schedule like a contract. Your first contract is simply your first semester. You might sign up to take four to five classes and make a commitment to go for a few months. Instead of the 24/7/365 commitment the military demands, you only have to be present in class for a few hours a week. It pales in comparison. In your mind this might even be a trial period, something to dip your toes into the water to see if college is for you. This is not the right attitude. That approach isn't going to cut it and will make it easier to quit when you get overwhelmed or challenged. Which, at some point, you certainly will. Push all the chips to the center and go all in, don't half-ass it.

Similar to combat, act like your life is on the line because in some ways, it is. I didn't think college was for me. I had failed out of college twice before trying to go a third time. It wasn't that I thought I was a total idiot, I just figured there were some people who were made for college and some that weren't. When I saw the other kids in my class, it seemed clear to me that they belonged there and equally obvious in my mind that I didn't. When I got into it though, I realized I belonged at college more than the other students. I had earned the right to be there, my college was paid for by my sacrifice to the country. For the other students, college was paid for most often by their parents. If you fully commit to college in the right way, I promise you won't fail. You might succeed beyond your wildest expectations if you do the right things. You might have to work a bit harder, but learning and college is for everyone who wants it. Just like anything else in life.

More and more professions require a college degree to even sit down for an interview. Just being a veteran isn't going to get you that job. Let's be real, some employers don't even want veterans, despite what they might advertise. Your level of education is going to correspond with your future success. People with college degrees rarely end up poor or homeless. Most people understand that the more you learn, the more you earn. The more years of education, the more doors open up, whether it be an associate, bachelor's, or master's degree. You've actually demonstrated your intelligence and proved yourself capable if you have a college degree. Additionally, college graduates usually have better communication skills, which has far-reaching benefits in employment and in life. As a college graduate you will know how to read and write effectively and how to speak intelligently. Lots of people are hired for good jobs straight out of college because employers look for new hires at the colleges. Did you see people lining up to hire you for high-paying jobs when you got out of the military? Probably not unless you had a special skill, specific training, or connections. I was an infantryman, and nobody cared that I could disassemble 50cal machine guns or set up ambushes.

I wanted to end up as a teacher because what I loved about the Army was getting to instruct and train motivated junior soldiers. I liked being able to explain things in ways that people understood, and I felt passionate about training life-saving or life-taking skills into my soldiers. I needed to go to college to do this and to be competitive against other teachers for job opportunities, I needed to do well. That's what led me to treat college like my new contract.

Your oath of enlistment in the military wasn't just for basic training or a few months. It was a years-long commitment with physical, mental, and emotional sacrifice. Then at the end, you can walk away, with experience, training, skills, and the many benefits military service provides. Look at college in the same way. The major difference here is that nobody pushes you like they did in the military, nothing's mandatory. It is up to you to be your own motivator and not give up when you get the urge to throw the towel in. There is no first line supervisor mentoring you and coaching you along the way. There is no drill sergeant yelling at you to do better or improve yourself. There are no formation times, and there's no strict accountability. There is only you, and if you think of college as a contract, then you will better stay on top of yourself. Taking orders is easy, but giving yourself orders and listening to yourself is complicated. No one is going to write you up if you are late or skip class, and no one is responsible for your successes or failures except for you. The commitment should feel the same, just as binding. Thinking about college this way will help get you up off your ass to go to class.

With your experience, you know firsthand the value of hard work. Martin Luther King, Jr., said, "If you can't fly then run, if you can't run then walk, if you can't walk then crawl, but whatever you do you have to keep moving forward." When I was trying to do college math, I had to learn things that weren't even being taught in class to understand what was going on in class. It was all nonsensical numbers and formulas to me, but the other students had already mastered the content. I realized this when we were on step three of a problem and I didn't understand where the hell steps one and two went. The entire class was running, and I felt like I was learning how to walk surrounded by a bunch of kids that had just done algebra last year in high school. I didn't even know how to multiply/divide fractions. I forgot what the hell exponents were! Why are there so many letters in my math problems? I'm not sure if I ever knew how to factor numbers. I looked at these problems, which apparently were "equations," and felt so lost and dumb. That really made it difficult to be motivated to go to class. I dreaded it, it was torture. When I went to tutoring, I had to put myself through an entire semester's worth of work to understand a quarter of what the professor was even talking about. I was sitting there for hours getting tutored by some eighteen-year-old math nerd. It was hard to go ask for help, but my commitment overrode my embarrassment. Veterans will run across battlefields to help a fellow soldier but struggle for asking for help for themselves.

I knew I really needed tutoring, but it was embarrassing in a way. It can be tough for veterans to ask for help. The kid was great, he explained things to me and didn't make me feel like too much of a moron. If I hadn't swallowed my pride by asking this kid for help, I might have failed this class or quit on college. Asking for help isn't a sign of weakness. You ask for help if you want to one day be strong. This is the dedication you might need to take to certain subjects. I told myself that I'm just not a math guy before realizing I hadn't ever studied math. I just copied off people in high school. Of course I didn't know what the hell I was doing; I had never truly put the effort in. I put in work when it came to my military contract and learned brand new, totally alien things. You put in similar efforts. I had to take that mindset of 100 percent commitment and apply it to college to win.

I'm still not exactly a math genius, but I trained my mind to be good enough to get by in that class. In so doing, I demonstrated my commitment to my college contract. I was prouder of that grade than I was of higher grades I received in other classes that took less effort. I didn't consider quitting or dropping the class as an option, just like I couldn't quit or drop the Army. If I had accepted that it was okay to drop the class, then I might have. I was struggling. After meeting lots of successful people, I realized this is what sets people apart: commitment.

The most successful people are committed to their craft and don't quit when they suffer setbacks, even serious ones. Successful people put in the hours required. If I took my commitment to college as solemnly as I took my commitment to the military, I could kick ass.

I wouldn't do the minimum. The minimum wasn't ever anything that would get you awards or get you ahead in the military. You know that you shouldn't just meet the standard, your goal should always be to exceed the standard. I wouldn't barely pass, if the professor said the minimum was a five-page paper than I would mentally commit to writing at least eight pages. If I thought I needed to study for two hours, I would double it to four. I was an infantryman in the Army, and I took my job seriously because lives—my friends' lives—relied on my performance. I wanted to take college as seriously as I took my combat job in the military.

In the Army, someone pounds on your barracks door in the morning if you didn't show up for formation. If you don't show up to your 0800 college class, no one is even going to likely notice or even care. You are an adult, after all, even if the military didn't always treat you like one. You aren't a member of a team in college. It is an individual game, although collaboration will benefit you. Getting your degree can feel endless, tiresome, and sometimes amazingly boring. If you have that false belief that boredom ends once you're out of the military, think again! You thought the endless waiting and the occasionally downright stupid things would finally be over once you became a civilian? Nope. Now you get to look forward to sitting through a three-hour lecture with a mind-numbing professor who can't even get excited about their own material. Similar to military life, there are going to be days when you're feeling low, exhausted, and beat down. Veteran dropout rates are high. Don't contribute to these statistics. In the tough moments, reach into your cookie jar.

Your "cookie jar," a strategy I'm referencing from famed Navy Seal David Goggins, is designed to push you through those times when you feel low and beat down. College is frustrating, sometimes super fucking frustrating, but inside your cookie jar are all those memories of when you overcame tougher things. The mental memories you have of dragons slayed, obstacles overcome, and challenges conquered. My cookie jar consists of times I felt like I couldn't walk another step in Afghanistan, when my back throbbed with pain, my feet were blistered and bleeding inside my shoes, and some Taliban fighters that were masters of hide-and-seek kept shooting at us. Some missions I didn't know if I would be able to make the dismount back to base, each step was torture. I survived seeing friends shot in front of me, seeing death on the battlefield, being blown up by IEDs, and going weeks without showering. These are the experiences that I thought of when I was struggling in college. Use your struggles as a personal reminder of your strength.

Your cookie jar experiences don't have to just come from the military. Hell, I've been divorced twice. I felt like if I could survive these various life challenges, then I could certainly survive writing a ten-page paper or taking a final. I believed that I could do it when I stepped back and thought about all I had endured and accomplished before I ever set foot in that college. Chances are you've dealt with your own tremendous challenges and survived. I survived growing up without a father, intense combat, and other struggles similar to what you have been through in your military and personal life. Everyone has a story, problems, and life struggles. Commit to self-development, not self-destruction.

Everyone fights battles every day, and it takes a certain level of maturity to understand that. You have cookie jar experiences your classmates don't have. You've been through suffering, pain, and discomfort that they can't conceptualize. Take these experiences and use them in your studies. If you've marched twenty miles with sixty pounds on your back in blistering heat or frigid cold, then you should be able to study for eight hours in a comfortable library or Starbucks before a test. You should be able to put in late nights and early mornings and double the efforts of the other students in your class when you need to. That'll get you ahead, I promise. You have real accomplishments, probably have a couple medals, some graduations, various awards and victories that your classmates simply cannot have. You need to use your experiences from your past contract to maximize your success in your new one.

You're going to do this in two ways, commitment and experiences. People fall short in college, especially in today's participation trophy world, because of a lack of commitment to their cause. College isn't hard; commitment to college is hard. Total commitment terrifies us, but everyone we look up to is obsessed with it. From Michael Jordan to Bill Gates to military members we idolize like Michael Murphy, these individuals embody true commitment. One of the reasons we remain scared of commitment is our fear of failure. I was really worried I would fail at college, that I just wouldn't be able to cut it in that environment. I thought that if I dropped out after being totally committed, then I would be a disappointment to the world, my family, and myself. If I only gave it half effort and failed, then it wouldn't feel like such a crushing defeat as it would if I gave it my all. What I'll promise you though, and what I came to understand, is that when you totally commit to a class, you aren't going to fail. This total commitment in your new contract means you have the dedication to do everything it takes to succeed. Like in your past contract, you have no choice but to succeed because failing isn't an option. Even if you fall on your face a few times, you are still moving forward. Just by undertaking college you are showing your pledge to your new contract and your future.

Commitment doesn't matter unless it's meaningful. It's easier to commit to having a few beers with friends than it is to spend your nights alone in a library learning math concepts. Especially when you haven't done algebra since the ASVAB.

Your classmates may have done math last year in high school or beyond your level, but they have never worked as hard as you. The only sleep they have been denied is when they stay up late playing video games. Your experiences of training, deployments, hardship, and a familiarity with pain trump their lack of real-life experiences. You can put up with a hell of a lot, which gives you a tremendous advantage over your classmates. You've been through adversity and come out stronger. The military wasn't exactly a walk in the park. Incorporating the toughness entrenched within you from your military contract into your college contract will give you the foundation you need to not only succeed but excel.

Understand your new battlefield environment

College lacks the structure that you've grown accustomed to after high school and the military. In college you might only meet once or twice a week, not every single day like back in your high school days. This means that in college you have to do more work outside of the classroom. No one is going to be there to hold your hand. With that being said, it's easier to forget material that you aren't continuously reviewing or building on each day. Professors typically won't review what was discussed last class, there is no check on learning to see if everyone is up to speed. When I had a week between classes it was difficult to stay on track, at least for me. The professors aren't monitoring your academic progress and won't call your parents or your military supervisor if you start failing. If you fail out of a military school, your boss yells at you, it's embarrassing, and they usually sends right back. That isn't the reality in college.

It is an enormous shift in learning environments since you're not just walking from class to class like high school. In high schools now, you can't even just walk out. You are closely monitored and there are security guards posted throughout most buildings. In college, that accountability is nonexistent. You can just walk out of class, get in your car, and drive away without anyone stopping you or caring for that matter. Nobody is going to declare you AWOL if you bail on class or dropout. No MP's are going to come looking for you. The personal consequences of breaking your college contract are only felt by you. You can't rely on your professors, parents, or administration. The only person that you can count on is yourself. The professors' only job is to teach the material, how much you learn is up to you. Don't be the student who's physically present but mentally absent.

In order to get to your ideal future and gain respect in the modern world, you must be educated. Malcom X said,

"Education is the passport to the future, for tomorrow belongs to those who prepare for it today." A college degree is almost a prerequisite for success in the modern working world and especially for specific professions that have degree requirements. To achieve the many goals you have, embrace your college contract like your previous military contract, with the same enthusiasm and commitment. You have taken your body past its perceived limits in the military, now is the time to do the same with your mind.

Military life, although challenging, is fairly straightforward. You know where you belong in the rank structure, you know what is expected of you and the measures of success versus failure. You know how fast you have to run, how well you have to shoot, or how you should perform at your job to be successful. You know what time to be there and what uniform to wear, there are regulations that dictate every action. You have a contract telling you exactly how long you'll be serving. In college, all that is gone. It is not as straightforward as the military but instead a more complex environment.

It's hard to understand as a student veteran just how in the hell you are supposed to fit in and what you are supposed to do. Like in the military, it takes time to get adjusted. In the Army, we would give "failure to adapt" discharges for people who just couldn't deal with military life. This doesn't exist in college, it's success or failure without much wiggle room. You either graduate college or you don't. With a focused military mindset, you can kill it in college. If you can survive military and college life and find success in both environments, then you are capable of anything. An accomplished veteran with a college degree is someone with unlimited potential, capable of taking on anything. This is your new contract.

SIT IN FRONT

"Ninety percent of success is just showing up. You're not going to feel perfect every day. Get there and start working."

Joe Rogan

After years of service, the military lifestyle became my norm, and in some ways it was my security blanket. I knew how to succeed, I knew what the repercussions would be if I screwed up, and I knew what to expect. Even if it was to expect the unexpected. My path within the Army was clear, there weren't many unanswered questions. In the military, options exist, but there's no question of how to get from point A to point B, the necessary steps are clearly outlined for you. "Keep it simple, stupid" is a phrase every military member is familiar with. I knew what to do if I wanted to get promoted or succeed. I could expect to be paid on the first and the fifteenth like clockwork. We weren't in control of our lives and that reality is comforting in certain ways. Once you get set in a routine, it becomes your normal reality. You understand it. Get up early, work hard, and go about your day listening to the orders of those appointed over you. Now there isn't anyone telling you what to do or how to do it, which is disconcerting for people when they get out. Or at least it was for me.

The military comes with built-in friends who all have similar values and qualities, mentors and leaders who are there to counsel and guide you, and tracks to follow for success. When I made the decision to walk away from the Army and start my life outside of the military, much like you have, I felt overwhelmed. The options are endless, the support system unclear, and the path to success a mystery. Nobody in the civilian world knows their place, whereas in the military you know exactly where you stand. What I did know for sure was the first step was college. A degree was required for my journey to be a teacher. I embarked on a new path, with no map, no clear guidance, only a known destination and a warrior attitude.

I showed up to my first college class fifteen minutes early and sat in the back corner of the room. I began to worry if I was in the wrong room. Literally nobody else was there and had this been an Army class, everyone would be there by then.

I started to get anxious when there were only five minutes left until the beginning of class and still no one was there. Either I was lost, or these kids were terrible. Good news, the kids were in fact terrible and they eventually began to trickle in, with more than half the class being late on the first day!

It was unbelievable to me at the time that they would be late on the first day. I figured it was just because it was the first day of classes but, in my mind, that was even worse. In the military, if you aren't early, then you're late. To be late the first day is an unforgivable sin. I hadn't yet shaken the military mindset where I felt most comfortable with my back to a wall, which was why I took a seat in the back corner. It's like showing up for a formation your first day in a new military unit late and unprepared, that isn't a good first impression and nobody is going to forget it. In my mind, everyone should have performed a reconnaissance mission prior to classes starting to confirm where they are located and how to get there from wherever you're coming from. It really blew me away that students came late to class every single day over the course of my first semester. How can you be successful in anything in life if you can't even be on time? In the military, we all learned to be on time, from day one. If you weren't, there were consequences. This is one of your strengths that seem simple to veterans. Professors do respect individuals that take their education seriously enough to come to class on time.

Picture this: day one of my college career and I am sitting in the back of the room, dressed in a tank top with shorts, lots of tattoos in full view, a full beard with a coyote tan assault pack sitting next to me. I wanted to blend in but didn't know how. For the last eight years I had worn a uniform every day. I felt isolated and out of place, like an adult sitting at the kids' table at Thanksgiving.

I soon came to terms with this. I would never appear as young as the other students and I could either be portrayed as the tattooed, bitter, and slightly threatening student veteran, or I could make the decision to put my best foot forward. Now, I won't tell you I stopped wearing jeans and a T-shirt to class sometimes, and I won't tell you I wore a suit every day. I did, however, make a conscious effort to present myself the way that I wanted to be perceived by my peers and my professors. If I was making a presentation to the class, I wore at least a shirt and tie. I took pride in my appearance, similar to my military experience. Think of people that just looked like hot garbage in their uniform. It affects how people treat you and their opinions of you. Veterans know that appearance is important, there are entire regulations concerning it. You aren't allowed to look like shit in your uniform, you aren't even allowed to be fat in your uniform in the military. Take pride in your class appearance, it helps set you apart as a serious student who is there to learn and graduate. This is another strength of yours over the other students who not only come in late but also look like they just rolled out of bed. Dressing like an adult will also give you self-confidence that will help increase your chances of classroom success as a student veteran.

During my first class, I noticed that as the professor spoke, the students half-heartedly listened. I probably spent more time during this first class watching the other students than the professor. Some were on their phones during class, some had Facebook up on their computers, and no one participated beyond the minimum requirement. One student even had earbuds in. I was appalled by this and truly shocked the professor didn't even seem to mind. One student came into class with nothing, no backpack, pens, laptop, absolutely nothing! In the military, if someone was in front of a room giving a class you were expected to have a pen and paper out, you were required to sit up straight, pay attention and engage with the instructor. If you didn't have a pen and paper out or even with you, you'd better be prepared do some pushups!

Not only did I have pens, I had twenty extra pens in case one didn't work, plus highlighters and notecards and all this other stuff I might need. That student that came in with nothing would have been smoked into oblivion for being so unprepared for a class in the military. I sat in this class, realizing that I was the only student even attempting to take notes (in my fancy brand-new notebook I had gotten from Target) while the professor taught. Even stranger to me was that a lot of students frequently left class during instruction or left early. The classes are usually a little over an hour. You're telling me they couldn't sit in a chair for an hour without needing to go to the bathroom or take a break?! I had been bored sitting in chairs or standing in lines for hours upon hours in the military. I could certainly sit in a desk during a class.

Again, this is one of those strengths I keep mentioning you have over the other students. You have mental and physical endurance for things that you may not be thrilled about. The military has taught us patience that modern students DO NOT have. You aren't going to miss anything if you stay in class for the whole lesson. You are dependable enough to show up to every class as well as not to not give excuses about being tired or sick. If you are anything like me, you may have shown up to work in the military hungover a few times but still on time, just maybe a little worse for wear. I couldn't be sick in Afghanistan; it just wasn't an option. Even if I wasn't feeling well, I pushed through just like you did.

I learned in the Army and it was reinforced in college that excuses always sound best to the people making them. Students would come to class twenty minutes late with a Starbucks cup in their hand and complain about parking. Okay, bro. It doesn't take Sherlock Holmes to figure out you are late because you went to Starbucks. You need a caffeine boost to pull through an hour-long college class you are paying thousands of dollars to attend, I don't. And as a veteran you don't either. The professors are not blind to this. Showing up early, staying through class, and not walking out during it will demonstrate to them the type of person you are.

As I looked around, I noticed that these students seemed like babies to me. At thirty I had gotten divorced twice, shot people, been shot at, and travelled around the world to places they probably couldn't find on a map. We can agree military life makes people a little rougher around the edges than most civilians. I continued observing the other students my first day. Most seemed like aloof rich kids fulfilling an obligation with their expensive laptops and Starbucks cups. I quickly learned that this wasn't the military anymore, and I just needed to adjust. At this point, I wasn't sure what kind of college student I was yet, but I was damn sure I wasn't going to be like these kids. Not surprisingly, I felt alone and out of place. As you might expect, my military mindset hadn't gone away, so as I observed my new peers and the professors who held the key to my future I asked myself a few questions: How can I succeed here? What is my competition like? What are the rules and regulations that I must follow?

The answers were simpler than I could have imagined. I flashed backed to being in an Army classroom and decided that I could use the same tactics that I had learned in the military to succeed here. I quickly ran down the list of requirements: show up on time (early), maintain your military bearing, show respect, come prepared and work hard.

In true military fashion, the next day I sat in the front, right in the middle with my notebook, pens, and highlighters at the ready. I quickly discovered that with zero distractions in front of me I could focus all my energy on what the professor was teaching. I couldn't see the other students browsing Instagram or Facebook anymore; therefore, it didn't affect me. When I looked at this college classroom using my military brain it began to make more sense to me. Something kind of clicked in my head that gave the class a sharper purpose. Everyone else could view the class how they wanted, but I wasn't going to fall into that trap. I had worked for years for the benefits and the right to sit in that class. I had seen people in the Middle East strive for the education that these "kids" were taking for granted. While their parents were paying for their education, they were viewing it as a simple box to check off on their pre-made life to-do list.

I decided that I was going to sit in front, pay attention, and take full advantage of this opportunity. Later, when I told a professor that I always sit in front, he informed me that according to research, students that sit in front get better grades than students that sit in the back. Knowing that, I wondered why anyone would sit in the back of the room. It simply helps you pay attention and minimize distractions. It demonstrates to the professor that you give a shit. There is also no way you're going to pull your cell phone out and text or get on social media during class if you are up in front maintaining your military bearing. You are going to sit up straight in your seat, pay attention, take notes, and show respect for the professor's experience as well as the material. If you do all those things you also will be able to better absorb the material, which will give you a better chance to be successful. Students who are constantly on their cell phones during class are not learning. As you would do in a military class, put your phone away.

I quickly learned that just taking notes was not enough. I couldn't possibly write down everything the professor said, and I had to prioritize what to write. Write shit down, don't just type it or text it in college. The pen is mightier than the keyboard even in the digital age. When you are sitting in front in your class, if possible—and certainly in your undergrad classes—put away your laptop and phone and take hand-written notes. Your computer can distract you in the same way your phone does. The laptop seems like the perfect tool for your classes. Yes, you can type faster than you can write and you don't have to worry about reading your handwriting, but research indicates that the simplicity is the problem with typing.

In order to learn you must be challenged, mindless activities don't teach us anything. With a laptop, you can mindlessly plug away or record whatever the professor says, but taking notes by hand forces your brain to work. You're processing the words and ideas where you can distill them into your own words. Writing things down is a more complex task than typing because it requires mental connections to move the pen and think about what you are recording longhand. Pressing a key is much less complicated since the computer will even fill in words for you, further eliminating critical thinking. With a paper you have more freedom, not less. You can cross things out, circle, underline, and write in margins, even draw pictures, charts, and webs to connect ideas. I would commonly draw arrows on my notes when things led to other things or were influenced by previously discussed material. I could add emotion when I wrote, emphasize things I found to be important, or even interesting enough to research later.

This simple adjustment certainly helped me, and writing things down will help you remember the concepts in class with more precision and clarity. It forces you to think about the material. Another way to retain the information being taught is recording lectures. I had some issues with my memory due to TBI (traumatic brain injury), and I found recording lectures helpful at times. I could record it and then play them in my car on the drive to or from school. This might seem like too much to some people, but it's like seeing a good movie again. The second time you watch it you catch a lot more of the things you missed the first time. It's the same with listening to lectures, especially test reviews. Everyone learns differently, some are auditory learners and listening to material again will allow them to gain a deeper understanding. Your time will be better spent listening to educational material rather than Lil Wayne, I promise.

If you sit in the back of the room and come unprepared to class, it's easier for your mind to wander, to lose track of the lecture and be disengaged. Being disengaged or distracted in combat can have tragic results. This wasn't combat, but I thought of the classroom as my new battlefield. With that mindset, I flourished in ways that I didn't think were possible. I became zeroed in on my education by showing up on time (early), maintaining my military bearing, showing respect, coming prepared, and working hard. Once I was mentally locked on my target, nothing could stop me. If you keep this mindset the same will be said for you.

VETERAN GRIT

"I don't lose any sleep at night over the potential for failure. I can't even spell the word."

James "Mad Dog" Mattis

Veterans possess a special quality that most of American society does not have. Grit, the spirit of an indomitable character, and the ability to persevere through hardship. A willingness to commit to something greater than themselves, no matter the potential cost. This contributes to something that defines all extremely successful people, the ability to outwork the individuals around them. I had something the other students in my classes could not have: resilience, work ethic, and mental toughness developed over the years. I had experienced combat, training, and deployments and had sacrificed in ways my classmates couldn't conceptualize.

In college, comparable to the military, the people that discover success are not necessarily the smartest. Instead, it's the students who work the hardest. This is the absolute best predictor of success. You aren't going to be the smartest student in every classroom, and I never thought I was. It takes grit to look hard at your reflection throughout your years in college and to keep going each day, even when it gets hard, which it will.

Before joining the military, I thought intelligent people were consistently successful. In the Army I learned that hard-working people were even more successful. If you think of the smartest people you know, they aren't necessarily always happy or prosperous. The people that aced the SATs in high school didn't always become millionaires. College classrooms are full of smart people, especially at great schools but intelligence doesn't directly mean success. Hard work corresponds with financial and personal success a hell of a lot more than anything else does. If you believe this, like I do, then you can achieve the success you desire in college through hard work and more hard work.

Moment by moment you are either moving toward your objective or away from it, the direction is up to you. Your movement will be a reflection of your actions day after day. If you have enough bad days in a row, you'll see yourself drifting farther and farther from your desired goals. You have worked hard for years in the military; you know how to be tired and keep going, because you've done it in more challenging and punishing environments. At times, you will have to work harder than the other students in order to catch up to their academic level after taking a break from school during your military service. You might have to suffer a bit, but difficult roads lead to beautiful destinations.

My suffering came within the first few moments of my first Spanish class. I had forgotten all the Spanish that I had learned in high school, minus *hola* and *cerveza*. I had the cerveza thing down but that didn't seem to help me much in class. The other students had just taken high school Spanish and I felt hopelessly behind in trying to learn and catch up. I almost dropped the class after the first day. I ended up with an epiphany after I thought about the grit that the military had ingrained in me. I couldn't take a pill and increase my IQ or learn Spanish in a day, but I could work my ass off. By the end of the semester I knew more than when I started. Not even just about Spanish but about myself and what I could accomplish when putting forward incredible effort. I got a tutor, worked on my study habits, did all the extra credit I could, and maintained my military work ethic throughout the semester. This provided me with the realization that studying hard was more important than being smart to get good grades. The other students knew more than me the first day of class, but I managed to finish ahead of them by the end of the semester. Not because I was smarter but because I worked my ass off.

Grit must be developed over time, and as a veteran you have already at least partially cemented it into your personality. Anyone who has successfully completed an enlistment or career in the military has done so because they had the grit to do so. Likewise, in college those who have successful academic careers have them because they work hard. Your effort is going to influence your success in college more than your IQ will. Someone who is more intelligent than you but puts in half of the effort you do won't kick ass the way you'll be able to in college. When you work hard and accomplish things, especially things that require grit, it gives you pride and a sense of victory wherever you are, the battlefield or the classroom.

In my high school locker room, our football coach taped up the quote "Hard work beats talent when talent doesn't work hard." This always stuck with me and I carried this mentality into the military. I tried to make sure I was outworking my subordinates, peers, and superiors. I wasn't ever going to be the most talented or gifted soldier or athlete, but I could control how much effort I put into things, even small tasks. The small tasks make up the big ones and if you are brilliant in the basics then it'll show in your end results. When I paid attention and did well on the little assignments like the homework and the quizzes, the big things like midterms and finals fell into place. Lots of student veterans will ignore the little things like the five-point homework assignments, but by the end of the semester they add up. If there are extra credit opportunities, do them. You are in complete control of your effort and attitude during this new journey of college. Work hard on the little things. I did, and you can too by tapping into your veteran grit.

Angela Duckworth coined the term grit. She defined it as "passion and perseverance for long-term and meaningful goals." The fact that it needs to apply to long-term goals is important, because school can be long and boring. Your major should be something you are passionate about, and this passion can propel you through the boring parts. As a veteran, you have had many hours of practice at being bored. I couldn't even add up all the hours I spent bored in the military, on endless guard duties or sitting around waiting for something. We have waited in lines for no reason, we've hurried up only to wait. You possess the ability to put in long hours studying things that aren't necessarily captivating but are important to your end goal. We know how to sacrifice.

Grit determines who is going to keep showing up, and as a

veteran you've showed up every day for years. A big part of being successful in life is just showing up. You have woken up at 0600 for PT formation hundreds or even thousands of times. You'll come to realize that showing up consistently for college surprisingly requires more self-discipline than you needed in the military. This is because there is no force pressuring you to be there. Whether you can be self-disciplined or not is going to make or break your college experience. There is no drill sergeant over your shoulder, you have to be your own drill sergeant. As Jordan Peterson would say, you must "treat yourself like someone you are responsible for helping." This change in structure leads to veterans dropping out of college because they can't handle the dramatic shift in schedules and lack of support. These veterans don't help themselves. The biggest challenge in college for veterans, including myself, is to keep going to class day after day.

You can't walk into college classes mentally defeated, just like you can't take a demoralized attitude into the military. I did this for a while in my math classes, walked in saying to myself that I'm just dumb at math and there was no chance in fighting it. It took me a while, a lot of talking myself up in the mirror, until I believed I could perform better in class if I worked hard enough. If I had maintained that self-defeating mindset that I had on my first day, I wouldn't have graduated college or even finished that first challenging class. One of the differences you'll see between the military and college is that you can't quit on the military, but it is effortless to quit on college. You can drop out pretty much whenever you want, you can skip classes and you can put forth almost no effort. Obviously, you know this is a no-go in the military.

The bottom line is when it comes to college, the only person that is going to be affected is you. What are you going to do when things get bad, when it gets harder? Because things will get harder in college and in life. There is no denying the tough days ahead of you. Your classes will get harder as you go on. My freshman year I could get away with drinking on school nights or half-assing it, but by the time I was a senior, that didn't cut it. You should do the equivalent actions that you performed in the military. Find a way to get it done, whatever the effort required. You have been to hell and back already, use that experience to rise to this college challenge.

Your inner voice is important here. What you tell yourself is going to end up being your reality. When I repeatedly told myself that I was dumb in math, guess what? I was dumb in math. When I changed my internal conversation to, *You are not naturally talented at math but with hard work you can pass this class,* my grades improved. Optimistic thinking in your own head will translate into better personal actions and a healthier mindset. Examining your own self-talk will help you out in your classes, in your relationships, and in your life. Just like in the military, you did things that seemed like the most idiotic things you can imagine, but you did them all the same. Sometimes you need to fake it until you make it. You know how to struggle, you have practice in it. Sometimes you need to have the grit to suck it up and do what must be done, even if it takes everything you got.

Evaluate yourself like you are your own subordinate and be honest about your strengths and weaknesses. It was easy for me to point out what I was bad at. It was more difficult to point out what I was good at. You should orient your major towards your strengths. I wasn't going to be a math or Spanish major. Do what you're good at in college, there's no reason to reinvent the wheel. Aside from honing in on your strengths, you should aim for your passions. I might be passionate about football, but I'm never playing in the NFL. I looked at myself and saw a combat veteran with some PTSD and some issues to work through if I was going to make it in college.

I knew I was talented at teaching military tactics and marksmanship but being a good teacher for civilians is very different. You have to be "nice" to people in the civilian world! You are going to have similar struggles, you might be good at things that don't translate well to society. Whatever MOS you had, you had specific training in it that was designed to benefit yourself, the team, the military and the country. My first squad leader in the Army made me take apart my machine gun hundreds of times and do drills with it until my hands bled. I lay in the dirt with him sitting on a stool next to me with him yelling, throwing rocks at me, and giving me firing commands on a shooting range. He taught me that stress must be induced into training because combat is stressful. I hated him for it at the time but when we saw combat and when I had to fix malfunctions and fire back, I rocked it. This was due to his hours of relentlessly training with me. Even if the training felt like punishment at times, it was valuable. You've dealt with stress in the Army and in life and death situations. You can deal with it in college.

In the civilian world, I couldn't exactly treat seventh graders like that when I was student teaching, even though some of them certainly needed it. That is one of the interesting things in the military opposed to college. In the military if you don't do it right the first time, you just do it over and over until you eventually get it right. Unfortunately, it's not like that in college. If you hand in a paper and it sucks, you just get a bad grade and that's it, you move on. In the military you would do it over because in the military doing things wrong can mean people getting hurt or dying. If you treat college with the same attitude and intensity, you'll figure out how to be successful. Even if it means doing something over and over again until you get it right, just like in the military.

Figure out your strengths to know what direction to go in and then floor it. Yogi Berra said, "If you don't know where you are going, you'll end up someplace else." Think realistically about where you're presently at so you can be where you belong after graduation. Figuring out how you learn best is going to impact your schooling. Some colleges act like there is only one way to learn, which is sitting passively in a large lecture hall with a professor blabbing on for hours. You know that isn't always the best way to learn, and you might learn more effectively in a different way. You can't learn how to handle a weapon from reading a book, you have to repeatedly practice with it. As a military person, chances are you learn most effectively experientially. Your experiences are what provide you the most educational benefit, actually doing things not just quietly listening. That is why some people who do amazingly well in the military end up failing at college. They thrived under that highly experiential nature of military learning and fall apart when they are forced to learn differently. I'm talking about the crawl, walk, run method where you do it all step by step, not simply by reading about it in textbooks. Veterans typically learn best by being as active as possible in their own learning, so you should really get after it. You need to be willing to try out different learning strategies to find what works for you.

You are essentially starting a second career and taking a chance to better your life by making the decision to further your education. I was nervous about starting school because I had literally been to two community colleges and felt like it wasn't for me at the time. Starting a second career takes guts and grit. Guts to have the courage to do something that might be out of your comfort zone and grit to have the perseverance to get it done. Fear is a normal part of life and is useful, even necessary in certain situations. That fear can help motivate you, but it can also hinder you. Not everything in life is going to burn you, and you are going to have to risk being burned to get anything worth having. Be willing to take some chances. One of these risks, a big one, is college. You have demonstrated both guts and grit as a veteran, and faced fear. Fear of the unknown and the real fear of dying or killing for your country. You have substantial skills that you shouldn't underestimate.

These learned skills will give you a wide range of opportunities after college too. At the end of the day when people look at you, they either see a winner or a loser. You signed a contract with yourself to complete college, but academic success doesn't come just because you wished for it. Other people aren't going to see the price you paid, the sacrifices that made up your time throughout college. You're the only one that'll appreciate the late nights, stress and commitment that you put in. Just as civilians can't understand all your military exploits, military people won't understand the college challenge. You have got to make it happen for you, using the grit you fought to learn in the military. Then you will come out of college with the degree and the skills necessary to live the life you want.

In your military experience, you saw the effects of people not having the necessary grit. They suffered, fell out of runs, failed out of schools, or were booted out entirely. I had a guy in my platoon during my first deployment shoot himself in the foot to get out of there. We were in a hard-fought combat arena and he couldn't take it anymore. Now his foot looks like a ninja turtle foot because he couldn't persevere through the long deployment. We got back after a tough combat patrol and were going to go out on another one in a few hours and he just blasted himself right in the foot. It scared the shit out of everyone because we thought we were under attack. I saw people get kicked out for drugs, going AWOL, DUI's, and failing to adjust to military life. I'm sure you met a bunch of these types of people in the military, maybe not ones that intentionally shot themselves in the foot but people that were out of their depth.

On the other hand, we've all seen people who endured far worse and rose to the challenge. A guy in my student veteran club at college lost his legs in Iraq, another guy I work out with lost his vision, but they maintained their sense of humor and winning American attitude. Veterans have a dark sense of. humor. Anyone who has been through basic training, deployments or spent years in the military knows this. This is the ability to look at the worst situations imaginable and make light of them at times to preserve your own mental health. Sometimes it's just how you deal with shit, veterans have always done it in every conflict mankind has fought. I had to put bodies in body bags that were hardly recognizable as humans. The smell of the charred bodies is something you never forget. My buddy in my platoon was helping me and he grabbed two hands. They looked similar to the hand in the Adams family, just somehow perfectly preserved to the forearm. He looked at me with a blank look in his eyes and then clapped the hands together. It was so shocking and horrific but at the same time it broke the somber mood and I couldn't stop laughing. It was nightmarish and one of those times when you don't know whether to laugh or cry witnessing the horrors of war. Veterans have a unique ability to mentally handle the worst of humanity because we are the ones on the front lines of the world's worst problems, from disaster to warfare.

I saw people fall apart at the smallest of obstacles and saw others refuse to stop hunting success, even after losing their legs, vision, getting shot, or more. Nobody really understands how resilience and grit work, but we do know they are both skills that can be improved upon with focused awareness. More than your experience, education, IQ, family connections . . . grit and resilience will determine who succeeds and fails and to what extent. This holds true in the military, in college, in sports, and in professional life. Resilience and grit aren't fixed qualities that you are born with, they can be built up over time. To build on these skills it is vital that you accept reality. You can't have the attitude that things are always going to work out in your favor, because you know life isn't like that. Instead you need to create situations that lead to your success.

Reality can be tough to face, even for veterans. When I got back bad grades in classes, I had to be honest with myself that I wasn't working as hard as I should have or could have. Initially I blamed my teachers for not teaching the material well enough, or I blamed the test for being too hard, just about any other excuse to avoid taking personal responsibility. It was only when I accepted total responsibility for my grades that I saw them start improving. Honestly, getting bad grades suck for anyone, especially when it's unexpected. It takes maturity to then look at the grade candidly and be honest about what you need to do to improve. It took a bit for me to realize that I wasn't working as hard as I needed to or as efficiently as I needed to be to get the grades I wanted. You need to take total responsibility for yourself and real ownership of your grades and your future. Whether you succeed or fail at college is squarely on your shoulders.

It takes mere seconds to walk across the stage to get your diploma at graduation but years of hard work to earn that reward. Each day, every class and all your assignments count on the path towards graduation. It takes grit to play the long game in college just like in the military. The clock can move slow as hell in the military, especially during long training or deployments. My first thirteen-month deployment felt like two years at the time. Now, when I look back, it went faster than it felt in the moment, which was the same experience as college. It doesn't matter if you did four years or over twenty in the military, you have that veteran's comprehension of what commitment truly means. My proudest moments and triumphs in the military came from the hardest times. It is the same in college classes. You'll ask yourself if it's worth it at times and think about the easier things you might do if you dropped out of college today. I know there were times in your enlistment when you questioned just what the hell you were doing there. It will happen in college when you are studying or working on papers you don't even really care about. Math was like that for me. I just had to take one math class in college and was totally disinterested in pursuing anything beyond that. When times like this come, you'll think you could settle for any job that doesn't require a college degree, maybe even go back into the military. Anyone can graduate high school, it's almost a given in society. Not just anyone can serve this country or step up like you and I did. It takes a committed and strong person. You ought to apply this commitment you learned in the military to this next chapter in your life. You're a veteran with veteran grit, now use it!

DON'T BE AFRAID TO LOOK STUPID

"A certain degree of intellectual humility is a good thing."

David Petraeus

You're allowed to look stupid in college. In fact, I would encourage it. College is generally viewed as an opportunity for young people to discover themselves, and for you it's not that different. The main differentiation between you and your classic college student is that you can rediscover yourself, mold yourself further into the person you could be. You already know a hell of a lot about yourself, insight you've gained through your military adventures. It is perfectly okay to wander around college stupidly trying to figure out just how you want to fit into the world, how you want to change the world, what occupation you might want or your desired path in life.

College should be a time of experimentation for you just as it is for traditional students. I failed out of community colleges, so when I went back, I tried to capture some of the regular four-year college experiences. Some of my friends and I in the Student Veterans Association even went to MTV spring break. Who cares what people will think, you're in college and you should make the most of it every way you can. Who you were before starting college isn't necessarily gone, but a lot of your identity has been stripped away after getting out of the military. This is your starting point to building the person that you want to become. To do this, you should be willing to escape your military comfort zone and forgo trying to look cool all the time. There is undervalued benefit from forcing yourself to be okay with looking stupid, especially at college. Smart is the person that you can become if you are willing to pay the cost of looking stupid up front.

For what felt like a lifetime, all I knew was the Army. I had uniforms in my closet and an American flag on the wall and I was a proud member of the greatest Army on earth. The Army defined me and when I got out, I wasn't around my friends all day every day working and fighting with purpose. I shared so many meaningful experiences with my brothers and sisters in arms in the military all over the world for years. I suffered from a lack of purpose and direction when I took the uniform off for the last time. I had lost my structured military community and my friends. It was like when I took my uniform off, I also lost who I was. Like a lot of other veterans, I lost my identity. This is why military suicides remain high: the loss of community and the loss of purpose. You must regain these two things and you can do that at college, where you will initially feel stupid and lost, not unlike how you probably felt those first few months in uniform.

It is more useful than you might think to be willing to look stupid. How can you learn unless you accept you don't know everything? If you want to become a Jedi Master, you must first be willing to be a Padawan. I thought I was somewhat enlightened and educated. When I got to college, I realized there was a world of information out there that I had no awareness of. We all think we are smarter than we are. I knew a guy my first deployment, I'll call him Reggie, who is a Wiccan. That's a religion of sorts, in case you didn't know. He didn't care at all what other people thought. This guy took a literal wand out on combat missions. He would use his wand to control the weather, cast protection spells over us, and do all sorts of other things. One time during a firefight my rifle got shot, which is about as close as it gets. He told me after that he was chanting spells and that was why I was protected. I didn't want to jinx it, and the last thing I wanted was to get shot, so I had him cast more protection spells over me. Fuck it, it couldn't hurt and I never got shot, so who am I to judge? He certainly believed in it and I was more willing to look stupid than to get shot. Reggie was willing to look stupid for his beliefs, despite what other people thought of him, and it worked for him in life. He got out of the military and got rich, never caring what anyone thought. So, work your magic, Reggie. Be willing to look stupid for what you believe in, even if it is a little weird.

In the Army, my first commander said, "Private Davis, there are three rules in this company. The first rule is look good, the second rule is know what you are doing, and the third rule is if you don't know what you're doing, look like you do." I still believe in living by this in certain aspects of my life, but in college you ought to ignore the third rule occasionally. Never pretend in your classes to understand something that you do not. Rather, you should seek help and ask questions. Pretending to understand things you don't is really going to fuck you over when that test gets handed out and you kept all your questions to yourself. The value of college is that you go in generally stupid and incapable and emerge intelligent and capable, ready for the next chapter of your life. When your knowledge levels grow then your capacity for success will follow. If you already are intelligent and capable like you might be, then you will be even more so after college.

You can do far more things after obtaining the coveted college degree. Doors open when you have military experience plus educational credentials. College teaches you how to effectively think and speak, which is really what you are there for, that and the piece of paper that is your diploma. Things always sound better in your head than they do coming out of your mouth. Working hard in college can change it so the words coming out of your mouth sound as intelligent and confident as things seem in your head. You do this in class by speaking, thinking, and then reforming your thoughts after speaking, then repeating. In order to do this, be willing to sound stupid.

You should be willing to sound stupid not only in front of the mirror but also in front of your peers and professors. Get in front of the class and work on improving yourself whenever possible, debate your classmates, be a leader in the classroom and speak up. I've heard you can't learn anything if you're talking, but this isn't always necessarily true. You can learn how to speak and articulate yourself intelligently by practicing it. This will help you in job interviews, work environments, and even with friends and family. This period of your life can give you the time to look stupid. You are a student veteran, which is a worthy identity to have. In

the professional world, being dumb as shit can have consequences and in the military, it can get you killed. In college
it gives you an opportunity to learn. When you learn you
get better and that's the whole point of college. Within this
student veteran identity, you have an opportunity to thought-
fully turn yourself into someone you want to become. You
can take this time to forge yourself into a badass veteran with
a college degree, capable of infinite success. This creation,
like any personal transformation, requires you not to be afraid
to look stupid.

The fear of looking stupid is going to make you look kind
of stupid. Everyone is somewhat insecure, and much more
so than they let on. People truly fear looking dumb in front
of their classmates. I know I did at first, and it was hard to
shake. This fear for me was worse than the fear of being shot
at. I initially really cared what these eighteen-year-old kids
thought of me and was self-conscious in the classroom. It
was only when I finally opened my mouth and looked stupid
that I saw the value in it. I realized everyone is something of
an imposter around others in education, everyone's trying to
look smarter than they are. I asked a pretty stupid question,
potentially embarrassing myself to the professor after class,
and after about two minutes of him explaining this concept in
a different way I figured it out. Like holy shit, I was dumb and

now I'm not quite as dumb. There is a Chinese proverb that reads "He who asks a question feels a fool for five minutes; he who does not ask a question is a fool forever." It turned out no one else knew what the professor was talking about either; he brought it up the next class and everyone agreed that they didn't understand. So, when he asked if anyone had any questions and no one raised their hands—me out of fear and my classmates for probably the same reason—I assumed everyone understood but me. Later it came to light that basically no one in the entire class understood. We all just didn't want to be the one to admit it. Obviously, other students have the same fears as you do, probably even more so because they are still young and haven't done stupid things in the military. You should be confident enough to not be afraid to look stupid in front of the other students.

One advantage you have over your classmates is that you have looked stupid before. Everyone does for their first bit in the military or has at least one big mistake. I fell for the pricky seven prank at basic training. If you haven't heard of this, congrats. A drill sergeant asked me to go ask our drill leader who was a Sergeant First Class (E7) for a pricky seven. When you say this, it sounds like you're saying a prick E7 which I can tell you he did not appreciate. Instead, he called my entire basic training class of forty individuals over and smoked us for about twenty minutes, blaming the mass punishment on Private Davis. I was pretty humiliated. These were guys I was going to have to be with for the next thirteen weeks and I had just gotten them smoked. They forgot about it long before I did, realistically probably about five minutes after, but I felt guilty and stupid for weeks. It affected my self-confidence. I brought it up to a buddy there the next week and he didn't even really recall it. You are always your own biggest critic, so don't worry about what others might think of your questions. Everyone overestimates the extent to which their mistakes are noticed by others. I thought that everyone would think I was the dumbest person on earth, but nobody even remembered that it was me. If you are confused about something or want some advice, I guarantee other people are in the same boat. So, go ahead and ask away, moron.

You're in college, this is the place to look stupid and uneducated. That is why you are there, to change those things over time. Something to think about is that everyone looks stupid somewhere. If I was to hand my professor an M4 and tell him to hit a target 300 meters away, I would guess that he would probably look pretty stupid trying to load and fire his weapon, let alone clear a jam. Of course, he might surprise me and secretly be a sniper, but I doubt it. Don't forget your strengths, the things you are trained to do in the military that you are probably the only person in that room capable of doing. You are capable of doing things that no one in that room can do, and that should give you a measure of confidence. The classroom environment necessitates people looking stupid in order to improve. When you hand in a terrible assignment you should hand in a slightly less terrible one next time. That's improvement, and that's what learning is. Just because you failed a paper or test, it does not make you a failure in life or even in the class. It was one assignment. Grow up, you are going to have to deal with bad or disappointing grades just like you dealt with misery in the military.

Small-minded thinking will instruct you to try not to look stupid in front of others. Big thinking, big ideas will tell you that it is a requirement. Anyone who had big ideas looked stupid to others in the beginning. If you ended up in the military, no offense, you've possibly performed poorly at academics in the past. This doesn't make you stupid. I failed out of two community colleges before the Army straightened me out. You know that there are different kinds of intelligence. In the Army, I was around genius computer programmers, talented medical personnel and master strategists. Some of whom could barely tie their shoes at times and couldn't kick in doors and clear rooms like I was trained to do. We each played our own part. Like guys and gals in your high school who could ace chemistry tests but couldn't talk to members of the opposite sex or pick up on obvious social cues. You and I both have different strengths to offer the world. Your life experience, your military experience counts for a hell of a lot. It is valuable, it provides you with wisdom, world knowledge, and practical skills. The nineteen-year old kids sitting to your left and your right have an experience deficiency. You are experienced in looking stupid and this makes you smart.

We all picture the worst-case scenario in our classroom environments, instead try to flip it. Picture the best possible outcome, not that the whole class will laugh at you and the professor will throw you out for your question. In my stupid questions I actually got smarter, pretty much every time. Every time I didn't understand something, or even only slightly grasped it, I raised my hand and asked a question. I would even ask the professor to explain it in a different way even if I thought I halfway understood. I'd pop in the professor's office during office hours and ask a few questions if they came to me. It showed the professor that I was willing to work at learning. This strategy led me to additional questions I didn't even know I had, which gave me a deeper understanding of a subject.

Step back and evaluate the bigger picture. If you stay within your comfort zone and only take classes you are knowledgeable in, you'll never grow. This is your opportunity to explore new areas, take a pottery class, an acupuncture class, explore Roman mythology and expand your mindset. But in doing so, you'll have to be willing to look stupid walking into a room knowing absolutely nothing. This could set off new passions, future career opportunities, interests, and hobbies. Maybe you are a master pottery maker. You have to run and mentally jump off the cliff that is your comfort zone, that's the only way you'll fly.

Introduce yourself to someone that looks smarter than you in your class. This is a solid tactic to boost your performance and increase your confidence in that specific class. You should be pursuing the best grade that you can, and this person most likely is too. Like you've heard before, two heads are typically better than one. This person can serve a bunch of purposes that can be mutually beneficial for the both of you. It is important that this person is reliable and committed to doing well in school. If you must miss class, if you get into a car accident or get sick, you want someone you can communicate with that can fill you in on what you missed. If you pick an ineffective student and then you text them for notes, you might find they didn't take any. Missing classes can have major negative effects and your partner can help you and you can in return in that class. School also gives you an opportunity to work on your interpersonal skills. When I got out of the infantry I legit could not speak without cursing, and conversations with civilians were tough. I had almost exclusively communicated with military people. Civilians are different. I felt like a citizen in a new country, immigrating into a more civilized world where I couldn't use fuck in every sentence. I introduced myself to a girl sitting next to me who, remarkably, turned out to be a Coast Guard veteran.

We had two classes together and held each other accountable, studied together, and even signed up for future classes together after our initial success. College can be confusing. Having someone who can be confused with you makes the experience at least more enjoyable. You can work on assignments together, bitch about professors, and study as a team. Having someone I trusted, especially a fellow veteran, gave me confidence. My Coast Guard friend would glance over papers for me and I would look over hers. We both understood veteran problems like the GI bill or the VA. Because of our collaborative relationship, we both did extremely well in classes we had together. We were something of a team. Being a part of a team is something you are used to and should carry on for your own sake. College doesn't have to be just a solo game, you can have teammates like in the military.

Being on a team means you don't do anything alone.

Incorporate everyone that can help you onto your college team. This might mean you look stupid, asking an eighteen-year-old kid something you feel like you should know. But it'll help your grade, and your grades matter. If you can't find a friend, get a tutor. Most schools offer tutors for free in an academic center on campus. I had tutors for my math and Spanish classes, both of which I struggled with. At the end of the college experience, what matters is that you were competent enough to graduate, not necessarily just your GPA. Shit, C's get degrees. It is about the experience, the learning, and what you can do with it. You'll be better prepared for your future getting C's but learning how to be an effective thinker, writer, and speaker than getting A's and learning nothing. Some jobs won't even ask your grades or GPA, but they need to see at minimum that you graduated. Grades are not the measure of your future potential. By looking stupid you'll have greater potential to get smarter. Don't be afraid to look stupid.

REACH UP AND REACH DOWN

"Lead me, follow me, or get out of my way."

George S. Patton

There should be at least two people who are going to be assets to your educational journey, who will carry you throughout your academic career and beyond. These two individuals don't have to remain the same individuals for your entire tenure in college, but you should always know who they are. They dually benefit you with contrasting approaches. One is a mentor. This person is someone you genuinely respect and admire and is typically down the road from you in life, meaning more accomplished. This person can be a professor, other faculty member, or more advanced student. Their presence, thoughtful advice, and genuine concern will improve your college experience and odds for success. On the other end of the spectrum, you want to find someone to mentor. This person is also someone you respect and can be anyone you believe your experience and advice will benefit.

My grandfather has been an avid member of Alcoholics Anonymous for over sixty years. His drinking got out of control when he was in Germany during his time in the military. He credits the individuals that he sponsors and being sponsored himself as the key to his sobriety and in turn his life success. In Alcoholics Anonymous you need to have a sponsor and be a sponsor, that's part of the program. He is ninety-one now and still has two sponsors that help keep him sober and still sponsors alcoholics. He continues to work to reach up and reach down, that's a winning veteran mindset. We all want to accomplish remarkable goals and reach great heights, but you won't get there going at it totally alone.

These binary relationships should ring true to the military mindset in that you always have someone in charge of you, possessing more experience, accomplishments, and ideally more intelligence and wisdom. Regardless of your rank or time in service, everyone is a leader in the military. You are always responsible for someone else and have been in leadership roles during your time in service. If you don't think that, then at least you can accept the fact you are in charge of leading yourself. Contrasting to the mentor rela-tionship, your mentee is behind you on the road of life but also someone you can be an asset to, possess respect for, and see your experience benefiting. These two relationships are therapeutic in that they create intrinsic feelings of value within yourself, make you appreciative, and help you gain self-esteem and confidence. They also have external rewards. You are much more likely to achieve your college goals if you take full advantage of these relationships. Success in life isn't for someone else, it is for you and your two mentor relationships. Focusing on this will drive you towards that success in college.

In college you are going to have to move toward self-reliance and create your own team, whereas in the military you were placed into an already existing teamwork system. In your military environment, no matter where you were, there was someone responsible for you. This person was responsible to lead you, coach you, guide you, and counsel you to be as successful at your job as you could be. Then someone was in charge of them, and so on. You had a chain of command who all had vested interest in your success and the success of the team. That has disappeared. The benefit of creating your own team is like the adage "You can pick your friends but not your family." You probably worked in the military with people you found it challenging to cooperate with. I know that I did. I spent seven years in the military and the morons that we give deadly weapons to boggle my mind at times. You know the type of guy or girl I'm referring to, think of your military past. How many privates do you know that bought a car with 25 percent interest, married a stripper, or did something else so dumb that it amazed you. Probably quite a few. I was in the infantry so I know at least fifty people like this, guys that couldn't manage their lives but somehow wound up in the Army, with weapons.

A necessity for creating your own winning team is a reliable mentor. This person is like your unofficial first-line supervisor. Navigating college life can be intimidating, challenging, and downright confusing. This person ideally has successfully been attending this school for a bit and knows the ins and outs, which can make their advice lifesaving. Your mentor can help you unfuck yourself when you start being your own worst enemy. It can be a professor, but I recommend an advanced student veteran. One thing I have noticed about successful people is they lift people up rather than push them down and they truly enjoy lending a hand to others. People who end up finding success have been routinely helped by others, so they want to pay it forward by reaching back and doing the same for someone else.

Successful people know the importance of building mentor and coaching networks. I mentored a few students throughout my college time, often in small ways and sometimes in very large ways. Everyone needs a brief reality check at times, some motivation, a pat on the back, or a kick in the ass. This is part of being a good person and friend as well as mentor. I went to college to be a teacher, so I offered to edit papers for student veterans at my school, specifically history papers, since history was my major and my passion. If you've ever read a Marine's writing, you know they need a bit of help (haha).

I was able to edit other students' papers in a cooperative way in which I could learn information while also becoming a better editor and writer and at the same time help them improve their own writing skills. I would frequently just ask my fellow student veterans if they needed any help with papers because I knew how hard it is to put your pride aside and admit you need some help. Don't be the type of person that needs to be asked to help your fellow veterans, reach out and help people because it'll help you. If you wait to be asked, it may never come.

I'll tell you this, in order to improve your writing skills, you have no choice except to simply write more and be willing to take criticism. You need be willing to take other people's feedback, just like in the military when people of more experience and knowledge would teach you. My first team leader in the Army made me stand in front of a mirror and say, "I'm not stupid, you are" for five minutes after a minimal mistake. Another guy in my unit named Private Carter had to carry a plotted plant around for a while in order to make up the oxygen he was stealing. He would take the plant to ranges, to physical training in the morning and to the chow hall. Even after he didn't have to carry it around anymore, he kept it and named it because he grew attached. The military is a weird world sometimes and everyone reacts differently to the military lifestyle.

The military tends to break you down a bit, and how you respond to that is going to dictate how successful you are in uniform. Your character—your patience for bullshit and your ability to take criticism—has been tested in the military. If your military experiences are in any way similar to my own, I'm sure you've been yelled at before and if you haven't, I doubt you were in the military.

Apply this ability to take criticism to your writing and schoolwork, both in your own mind, with your mentor, and when you get grades back from your professors. Your professor will provide you feedback on every assignment and you can take that to your mentor to discuss how you can best improve yourself. You can also sit down with your professor and discuss his remarks and feedback to apply to your next assignment. Professors eat that shit up when they give you specific things to improve and on the next assignment you improve that specific thing. Feedback and criticism give you clear guidance on how to boost your learning. When you get a paper back, don't just look at the grade on the top but instead read the comments, they are more important. They will help you in the future to be a better critic of your own work. Your advantage over your peers without military experience is your thick skin. They are unable to accept criticism, even from professors with expert knowledge about subjects. You should be willing to take your professors' and mentor's advice and criticism and to improve yourself and your college work. In contrast to your student peers, you were called worthless, and I'm sure worse, by a screaming drill sergeant or leader in the military. Don't shy away from criticism or feedback if you want to build on your strengths or improve upon your weaknesses.

We are all blind to our own weaknesses. Your mentor will point out the changes that you need to make to improve your work that you might not see at first. That's how you grow academically, by being willing to accept your weaknesses and face your insecurities. This requires you to be honest with your mentor, even with uncomfortable truths that can include PTSD, stressful home/relationship situations, and financial problems. Be willing to ask questions. These people have been in your shoes and can help you. The difference between your mentor in college and your boss in the military is that you can choose them and the spirit of your involvement. Your boss in the military might not have been your mentor, even though they should have been. They may not have helped you discover or create your best self and they could have even been toxic leaders. You can choose who you want to help mentor you, someone you respect and who you trust will be there for you. This college mentor is like a team captain, who can explain things in plain language and shorten your learning curve in college. There is a big learning curve in college for veterans. It took me a while to get into the swing of things and adjust to my new life. The first semester you are going to be a little lost figuring it all out, like I was, but your mentor can get you up to speed. Benjamin Franklin said, "Tell me and I forget, teach me and I may remember, involve me and I learn." Your mentor doesn't just order you around like your former military boss did but instead works with you to propel you forward collaboratively. Working together, you can really improve yourself by working closely with an intelligent person you trust. Your mentor is going to help you keep going when classes get hard, help keep you accountable and on track. They are going to call you out if you skip classes or party too hard while ignoring your schoolwork. You didn't want to disappoint your boss, commander, or supervisor in the military, and you won't want to let down your college mentor. They are working with you, shoulder to shoulder, to help you succeed by providing encouragement when you need it and a kick in the ass when you need that too.

Your mentor is also something of a sounding board you can bounce ideas off without fear of judgment or reprisal. You will have questions about advisement, where to get coffee during breaks, professors you should avoid, resources the school has to help you, and your future. They will have sound advice for you based on their personal and professional experience. College is a good period to figure shit out and in order to do that you have to ask questions and try new things. Your mentor is free. This isn't a drawback but instead an advantage in that they are helping you for their own personal growth and to look out for a fellow veteran. They know they should give back and pay it forward.

I have had several mentors, none of whom I have ever gotten down on a knee and asked, "Will you mentor me?" Instead these are people that I admired and looked up to for different reasons. I relied on them for help when necessary. They cheered for my successes and worked with me to reflect on my errors. My college mentor was a student veteran who was ahead of me and I would give her my papers to read over. The advice she gave was invaluable. She taught me how to use the library databases and take the right professors, as well as providing accountability that I desperately needed. She provided a trusted friend that I could talk to about my ideas, classes, frustrations, professors, and peers. I remember my first ever college presentation. I was nervous about getting up in front of my college class. She told me to practice it with her as the audience. When I did, there was some issues with my PowerPoint that I hadn't seen that would have caused me to lose points. If she didn't catch these mistakes, allowing me to fix it beforehand, then my grade would have suffered. When I spoke in front of her and listened to her feedback, I was a better presenter in my class and ended up with a great grade. Practicing also boosted my confidence. It was a great strategy to do a practice run. She also recommended that I dress up, because it would make my presentation more professional. I put on a shirt and tie, which the professor greatly appreciated and respected. Because of my mentor, I got an A. Without her I would have gotten maybe a B or C. This is a small part of the big difference a mentor can make for you. Even this minimal difference helped me be a better and more prepared student.

After seeing how my work improved after having someone look it over, I learned to never hand in a paper without having someone review it. I'll mention this a few times because I think it is very important for you to do. It was because of my collaborative relationship with my mentor that I was able to be very successful in college. I wasn't just blindly going at it alone; I was part of a team. I recommend you do the same. It can be difficult to evaluate your own work, but other people bring a unique perspective and feedback will improve your papers, assignments and presentations.

Your mentor provides you with encouragement, reduces your mistakes, builds your confidence, provides a resource for life, and increases your chances for success. In order to get help, however, you need to be willing to ask for it and you should realize we all need help. My Army mentors during my time in uniform have written strong letters of recommendation, advocated for my promotions, and given me military school opportunities. My military mentors when I was still in the Army saw that I wanted to improve and put in special time and personal effort to help me. On any level, motivated soldiers are what leaders want. Similarly, professors want motivated students who care about the learning process and desire to be better. Why should college be any different than the military? Get a mentor and kick ass.

On the other side, mentoring an individual will provide important opportunities for personal growth. Having a mentee can help you just as much as it helps them. Your mentorship to another person will certainly help them but it is going to help you as well. Your mentee will give you the excuse to sharpen your own communication and interpersonal skills. The best way to learn things is to teach them, that is why in the military they encourage all personnel to teach classes. My squad leader on my first deployment told me to teach a class on doing head space and timing on a fifty-caliber machine gun. I told him I didn't know how to do that. He explained to me that was the point and this experience forced me to learn not only how to do it but how to train others to do it as well. I had to learn it backwards and forwards to teach it to others. It was a great instructional tool. This strategy applies to mentoring as well.

I became a much more intelligent, capable, and overall better person when I started helping others. I spent hours in one-on-one counseling sessions talking and helping my fellow student veterans at college, over coffee or beers or whatever. These individuals did not just turn to me for academic support. Rather, my advice encompassed the variety of experiences that make up our lives. I had a few individuals I mentored where we would meet and they would share with me their frustrations with life, school, relationships, PTSD, finances, or whatever else came up. Unfortunately, in today's society it has become easier to criticize people than to help them. If you help people then it has a rippling effect across your little world, making it a better place. If you aren't making someone else's day better, then you are wasting your day. Buddha said, "Do good and good will come to you." I believe that. No growth comes from unconstructively criticizing others. I recommend you discard the military mindset to treat people like idiots, and instead treat them as what they could become. By empathizing with your fellow student veterans and working with them to help solve problems, you are forming support structures that will benefit your collegiate life and the lives of those around you.

I started college at thirty, but many people begin college at twenty-one or twenty-two, after one enlistment in the military, or after twenty years in or even after attempting to go into the workforce. Even as I was struggling in my classes, I found myself in a unique place to be able to use the combat leadership skills and life experiences I gained in the military to be a student leader at my college. Speaking with other veterans forced me to reflect on my life, share my experiences and pay it forward. Here I was, someone other people felt was trustworthy enough to confide in and intelligent enough to provide competent advice on different issues. It gave me a reason to push myself to be better, just like leading soldiers in combat. I gained purpose to push myself for personal, academic, and professional growth. I had to strive to hold myself to a high standard to maintain my status as someone other people could count on. This helped me maintain laser focus on my own classes and life.

It is easy to overlook the benefits of mentoring others in our gimmme society, where people only sometimes seem to care about what you can do for them. Often people look to friends for advice. I generally advise against this practice. Your friends are your friends. You should take academic advice from those smarter than you, business advice from those richer than you, and fitness advice from those that look better naked than you. This seems like common sense to me but often I would see student veterans turn to people worse off than them for advice. I would tell people, you shouldn't ask me relationship advice, I've been divorced twice before the age of thirty. Now on the other hand, if you want advice on how to pick up girls, I can help you with developing confidence and getting in shape. Think about the person you usually ask for advice. If you don't have that now is the time to find it. Honesty is an important quality to look for in both the person that mentors you and the individual you mentor. With veterans, the most insecure people will often act the most secure, the most ignorant will act enlightened, and the most out of shape people will give you advice on how to look good on the beach. You've experienced this and if you haven't, then you haven't opened your eyes to it and are maybe taking advice from your friends who are just as dumb as you.

Successful people do not hide from responsibility but instead take on more. Taking on a mentee gives you a chance to shoulder a heavier burden, to look out for someone academically, personally, and emotionally. College can be tough for veterans, that is why there is such a high dropout and failure rate. Having someone who counts on you forces you to be present and be a role model other people can depend on. When you give someone else advice, you can frequently see the big picture that they are too invested to see. Midterms and finals are the big execution moments in college, and the most important part of any mission is planning. Create a thoughtful timeline of studying around your midterms and finals with your mentor and for your mentee.

The mentor and mentee relationship, with you in the middle, will provide lifelong benefits for all parties. The person mentoring you will push you to be the best person you can be during college, show you the ropes of developing healthy study habits, provide future employment opportunities and empower you to reach agreed-upon goals. My mentor showed me the dean's list that my school posted with engravings of successful student names on the wall. She told me I should aim to get my name up there as she showed me her name up there. I had just been trying to pass my classes! I soon learned to expect more of myself, to work my ass off to get as much as I could out of the next few years at this school. Well, I got my name on the Dean's list, that semester and every semester after. I attribute that to lessons I learned in the military that I applied to college. Mentoring people provided me the opportunity to work on straight talk, to be honest with people while providing formative feedback. I learned to listen better. Most people don't communicate to really listen, they communicate to impress other people or be heard.

Learning how to really listen to people is an invaluable tool that can be applied to all aspects of your present and future life. When you really listen to people, they tell you the most interesting things. Be present in your mentoring relationships to gain insight into others and yourself. You should leave conversations with your mentor confident enough to be in a better place than you previously were, capable and ready to stand in defiance of whatever obstacles are in front of you. In the same manner, your mentee should leave conversations with you in a better place, feeling more confident. Reach up and reach down.

BUILD THAT RESUME

"Victorious warriors win first and then go to war, while defeated warriors go to war first and then seek to win."

Sun Tzu

More important than a diploma is your resume. Your resume is a snapshot of who you are and what you have done. Make it appealing and worth the read; it's the first impression that an employer has of you. The time to start creating it is not near graduation. You want to demonstrate that you got far more out of college than just a degree. Anyone looking for a job is going to need a resume, and I assume you fit in the category of anyone and will eventually one day require employment. The immense importance of your resume shouldn't ever be underestimated, it's going to be the bridge that connects you with a prospective employer. The hook that demonstrates the kickass human you are and makes them want to hire you right here, right now. This simple piece of paper is hugely important to your future, more important than it ever has been historically in employment. It used to just be something an interviewer would hold and ask you questions from while conducting an interview. Today, it is the resource that is going to get you in the door and sitting down in that interview. A great job opening is going to get hundreds if not more resumes in response to a desirable listing, and resumes are the only impressions they get of all the individuals hunting that job. The little piece of paper is going to be more important than your diploma, which maybe no one other than your mom will ever ask to see.

As opposed to other people who have talked about resumes with you, I don't think your time in college should be spent developing your resume as a piece of paper. I mean, I don't think you should be focusing on templates, trying to make it snazzy, thinking about cover letters, or trying to make it wow people with buzzwords. Instead, you should be focusing on creating meaningful content to fill up your resume. Everyone, for some mysterious reason, is interested in perfecting the resume as a paper instead of creating themselves into the perfect candidate. College is full of great opportunities to add substantial content to your resume. This is where additional endeavors come in, you need to get involved in other aspects of your school and take advantage of everything you can. I don't mean just hitting up college parties on the weekends. I joined honor societies, made the Dean's List, and involved myself in academic and volunteer clubs. All these things are going to make you more attractive to employers.

It seemed to me that other veterans at my school were overly concerned with constructing a winning resume. They wanted to create some magical Harry Potter resume that was going to get them every job they could ever want. I saw veterans being far less concerned with building content to make their resume more substantial, especially to civilian employers. This is stupid, you can do better. You have an allotted time where you are getting an education to be better prepared for your future, there is more to your college time than just the degree. Every day you have an opportunity to add experiences to your resume so when you graduate, employers will want to line up to hire you.

When prospective employers look at your future resume, as phenomenal as it might be with fancy fonts or whatever else, it's still about the content that constitutes it. Without real-world and practical accomplishments and experience, it just looks like fluff. Employers can tell when you are just using filler words to make up for a lack of meaningful work experience, volunteering, or education. You have years to create valuable and desired content that will enhance your resume and improve yourself personally and professionally.

The first thing you should do is demonstrate your involvement in meaningful things. The easiest thing you can do, without a major time commitment, is simply join a club. Getting active on your campus shows employers you are a passionate and enthusiastic person. Then you are beginning to put worthwhile words on your resume. Ideally, you get involved in a club that relates to your potential profession. For example, if you want to be a cop go join the criminal justice club. If you want to work in communications, then join the communications club. If you're a nerd, join a computer club, gaming club, coding, programming, or whatever you like doing that relates to your desired career. Clubs are going to give you an opportunity to learn more about your subject, as well as gain valuable connections, mentors, experience, friends, and possible employment. You'll meet like-minded people who can hook you up with employment opportunities during or after college that are within your chosen field. Even if you join a club that isn't related to your future profession, it still shows you are a go-getter and willing to take on challenges. You can also take a leadership role inside your club, which looks even better on a resume and demonstrates a willingness to take on responsibility.

I took on an officer position at my Student Veterans of

America club, and that experience improved my resume. It shows I'm willing to put in extra time and effort for a cause that I care about, helping veterans. If you're passionate about something and no club exists for that at your school, then create it. I don't know what you get fired up about, but starting a club or organization within your institution shows your willingness to take on projects you care about. If your chosen school doesn't have a Student Veterans of America chapter, then you can start one. That's pretty simple and obviously looks stellar on your resume.

The second thing you should do is volunteer. I'm not really trying to convince you to change the world or make an authentic difference, I'm telling you that employers want to see it on a resume. Don't just put it on there, though. You need to actually volunteer, obviously. It's admired and increasingly necessary to have on a resume. Volunteering tells employers you have a positive attitude and aren't just driven by monetary rewards. Just because you aren't getting paid for your volunteer work doesn't mean it isn't going to benefit your future. You develop skills while you are volunteering, especially if you find a way to orient your volunteering toward your chosen field. There are professional advantages to volunteering in your field, you can acquire experience that will put you miles ahead of your future competition. All jobs want experience, and college is an excellent time to get experience while volunteering. You can also engage in professional networking while volunteering and meet influential people in your field. These people can give you exceptional letters of recommendation or future references that can give you an edge in employment. Employers respect someone who is willing to volunteer at animal shelters or wherever help is needed. Maybe the person interviewing you is an animal lover and that experience will land you the job.

Volunteering can also help you figure out what the hell you actually want to do with your life. If think you may want to be a paramedic, go volunteer at an ambulance company or within the emergency medical field somehow. Then you can check it out and see if it's for you. It'll allow you to discover how you want to fit into the civilian world as well as how you must effectively work wherever you end up. If you volunteer, you are going to end up a more well-rounded individual and embody the whole person concept employers prefer. You'll be more confident and it lets you apply your skills with real world application. Volunteering is also just good for you. It improves your health and strengthens the community you live in, so get out and volunteer to build that resume.

The third thing I'm going to recommend that I've seen people find a great deal of success doing is landing an internship. It is also an ideal way to build experience in your field before you walk across the graduation stage. It can directly lead to a job offer at the company you are interning at upon your graduation, which I saw a veteran at my school do. He waltzed across the stage and got his diploma and went right back to where he was interning, making great money in a job he really enjoyed. They hired him because they knew him. It took the stress right out of the job search for him because he was willing to put the effort in to set himself up for success.

The college you go to should have a career office that can help you with internships, go talk to them. If they don't, you can search online or ask your mentor or even professors. A creative idea is to simply stroll into a company like you own the place and ask if you can do an internship there. Start your own position and gain the experience that you want. In doing this, you are creating your own internship, which is badass and shows you are a go-getter. The worst thing they can do is deny you. The great thing about internships is there is really no downside to it, you gain experience and can put valuable content on your resume after. Internships are often flexible and can work around a college schedule. That's what they are designed for, so don't be afraid to go for a position even if you think it's taking on too much. The internship is probably somewhat negotiable, especially if you are a quality candidate and a hard worker.

There are a lot of ways to make yourself more marketable during your college experience in addition to clubs, volunteering, and internships, but those are the big three. No matter what, you should keep records of everything you do, just like in the military. One of the unsurprising things you can do that is pretty apparent is that you can get good grades. A high GPA will mean something to your employers. If you earned a terrible GPA, don't include it on your resume. The common rule I've heard is that if you have beneath a 3.5, leave it off. A high GPA will also open doors for future scholarships and awards. It will earn you a spot on the Dean's List at your college, which is essentially an honor roll of high-performing students each semester. When I earned a spot on the Dean's List at my school and got a certificate mailed to my house, I gained a certain level of personal satisfaction and pride. I worked hard and it felt good to have that hard work get recognized. Some colleges have receptions to celebrate the Dean's List academic achievement of students and events like this can help you network. Once you get on the list and get that recognition, go ahead and throw it on your resume. It looks prestigious and adds something to your resume that other people might not have.

If you have a high enough GPA, in addition to the Dean's List, you should join an honor society. I joined the history and educational honor societies at my school because I was a history education major. Many honor societies are nationally recognized, and there is one national honor society specifically for veterans called SALUTE. I would recommend you join that as well, it cost forty bucks and they send you a certificate and a coin. To join honor societies, typically all you need to do is pay a small fee and write a short essay, provided you meet the requirements. It's extremely straightforward and looks extraordinary on your resume. It portrays you as a competent individual and sets you apart from other people. There really isn't much of a time commitment when joining an honor society. I'm in three honor societies and the only meaningful effort I've put forward was when I joined them. You can also meet new people in honor societies who will motivate you to perform your best.

In the military you want the best soldiers on your team, especially in combat. In college as well, you want to surround yourself with hardworking and talented people. My history honor society is all the best history students in my graduating class, so it is a smart group of people, the kind of people that I want to surround myself with. You should do the same. In the same regard, you should avoid lazy and unmotivated people.

There are employment benefits through honor societies alumni networks where they send you helpful and current materials in your field. My educational honor society sends me new information in the educational field and articles that benefit future teachers as well as current research. Honor societies are under-utilized at colleges. Fewer people are putting them on their resume or even joining, but they make your resume shine a bit brighter.

Studying abroad is another effective resume building option. I went to Thailand for an educational program and had an amazing time there, learning a lot about education and teaching. Every major institution has some type of study abroad programs, if you do one of those you gain valuable global experience to add to your military experience. If you already possess global experience in the military then this turns you into an even more attractive job candidate. Someone who has spent time in multiple countries is someone who is ready to tackle large-scale challenges in the workplace and connect with more people. You have to get ahead of them and demonstrate your real-world experience on your resume. The world is getting to be a smaller place and you can learn culture and language skills that will make you even more employable. For me personally, studying abroad was life-changing and opened my eyes to so many things.

It shows employers that you are adventurous, open-minded, and flexible and possess an expanded worldview. Seeing the world is a personally enriching experience, so if you have the opportunity to study abroad, I suggest you go for it.

The opportunities are endless, and the more creative you are with your experiences the more you will stand out when it comes time to compete in the job market. Think about the things your competition might write and make sure you produce a better product. You already have a leg up with your military experience. You have awards, deployments, training, and leadership skills that employers want. You can win that competition by starting now during college. Preparation isn't ever wasted time. The more planning and preparation you invest in during your time in college, the more success you'll find in the real world. The more time you put into working on your resume, which means working on yourself, the better it'll be when you are out searching for that perfect job. Build that resume!

POLITICAL PROFESSORS

"If everyone is thinking alike, then somebody isn't thinking."

George S. Patton

You had to work for a variety of people in the military. Some were tremendous leaders who inspired you to show up motivated every day to serve your country. You had diverse leaders, instructors, and teachers in the military, from your recruiter onward. All of them contributed to your military knowledge and career. You don't have to think too hard to imagine the bad leaders either, ones that demotivated you, created a toxic environment, or worse. There really are some of the best and worst people in the world in the military. College is no different. There is going to be a broad range of professors you are going to have during your schooling and your interactions with them can make or break your college experience. Just like your leadership in the Army, how you approach your relationship with your professors is important.

I have seen veterans blow up at professors, storm out of class, cuss out professors, and more. I've done it myself. At times it can be difficult for a combat veteran to be in a college classroom. There isn't anyone in the class that can relate to your life experiences, so developing friendships with the other students is tough. Before you ever get to your first class there are things you can do to set yourself up for success. The first thing you can do is ask people you trust, like other veterans at the school, the best professors they have had. Secondly, speak with your adviser and ask their advice. They are, after all, supposed to advise you, even though not all of them seem to be aware of that. Some student veterans never speak to their adviser or, worse, don't even know who their adviser is. I recommend developing a good relationship with your adviser. They can be helpful in ways aside from simply signing you up for your classes. You should work with your adviser to make a successful college strategy regarding your class schedule and course load all the way to graduation. If you show up for the first day and can't see yourself making it through the semester dealing with a professor, then quickly speak with your adviser. It's possible you can switch classes, but you have to seek out their help and support for setting up a schedule with your success in mind. Thirdly, look up your professors online, but be careful about reading too much into the reviews on ratemyprofessors.com. Some professors that I thought were incredible got awful reviews. Many times, the bad reviews were because they held immature students to high standards. Go ahead and check out the reviews, but don't live and die by them. The students who wrote negative reviews were probably the students who got the exact grades they deserved after putting in minimal effort. Not everyone deserves an A, just like not everyone deserves a trophy.

You also must think about your own learning style when selecting professors. How does this professor teach or grade, and what aligns most closely with your strengths? Trust your fellow veterans at the school and ask them and your adviser for assistance in making your schedule. Unfortunately, many times you don't have much flexibility in taking professors and get stuck in a less than ideal situation. I certainly did.

I had a professor my first semester who I legit just could not understand very well. His English was not good at all. There are quite a few professors like this, an increasing number of teachers are from foreign countries. Not being able to understand the teacher destroyed my excitement and motivation for the class, which I was legitimately interested in. I had to focus intently just to try to translate what he was saying and then convert it into notes that I could understand.

When we would walk out of class students would voice their frustrations to each other. Learning is already difficult enough without the language barrier. He used phrases and analogies that didn't make sense to us. Going to his office hours didn't help either, he was annoyed at having to re-explain himself, and at my confusion. I had to bust my ass in his class. Going to the class initially didn't really help at all but I still showed up every time. Many other students didn't. Over time, I understood more and more of his accent so I would recommend you stay patient and don't give up immediately. The instructor can also add diversity to the class from their global experience, which can be a beneficial aspect of a foreign teacher. I read the entire textbook, asked him for additional readings, and did research on my own. It wasn't easy for me, I had to put in extra effort, but I was willing to pay that price. I watched YouTube videos, spent hours teaching myself the material, and figured out that the class was going to take a hell of a lot of effort. A lot of students were so defeated by his accent that they weren't willing to give the class a chance and ended up with bad grades or dropping. I ended up learning a tremendous deal during the class by pursuing my own intellectual knowledge because the class time was next to worthless. On your GPA it isn't going to say you had a bad professor or you couldn't understand what they were saying. It's just going to display that YOU got a bad grade. Keep that in mind in these types of situations.

There is a power imbalance in college classrooms. What I mean by this is that the professor has the authority, the credentials, and power in the classroom. The students are uninformed, and the professor is there to make them more knowledgeable. From this perspective, the professor's opinions, thoughts, and ideas are superior to the students. This makes sense; the professor is more educated on the subject they are teaching. This doesn't mean they are right about everything, and some professors have a superiority complex. I have had professors who spent their entire lectures giving political speeches about whatever issues they were passionate about. Certain professors will say politically charged comments and even demonstrate anti-military sentiments. No matter your own political views, college is a place where the professors press down their views frequently. Combat veterans can struggle with this and being alert to it ahead of time will help you manage future frustrations. You might need to play the game sometimes. Let's face it, you worked with people you hated in the military and college is no different.

It isn't surprising to you at this point that most college professors are inclined toward one side of the political spectrum. I mentioned it to a professor once and he said that's because teachers were educated. It was a pretty clever response. Of course, the implication was that the uneducated were conservative and the educated individuals in American society leaned liberal. Some people will tell you that professors shouldn't talk about politics, but I disagree. Politics are an important part of our culture, especially recently, and people should learn how to have respectful disagreements and be open to new ways of thinking. Then when students go out in the world, they can understand that there are people of intelligence that possess good intentions on opposite sides of political issues. The problem in college classes is that students often do not challenge the professor's views, which usually emboldens them to say more and go further even to extremes. This is because of the power imbalance. Students don't want to get poor grades for disagreeing with the professor, even as respectfully as possible. This can be very challenging for veterans to deal with, especially when a professor's comments disparage the military, military service, or current conflicts. Thought diversity is an important aspect of college campuses, you should be willing to interact and have conversations with people that feel differently than you on certain issues. Often, the professors will casually say remarks that offend student veterans, but try not to take it too personally. Instead treat these comments as an opportunity for personal growth. I have combat veteran friends who have claimed grade discrimination based on their political views or veteran status. It is entirely possible for you to get a bad or lesser grade if you write the opposite political views of your professors on your papers or essays. If you get assigned to write a paper for a liberal professor that has strong views, it may benefit your grade by writing what they want to hear. This is just a fact of college. Unfortunately, I experienced this firsthand when I wrote a paper about immigration stating that a border barrier would equal less drugs crossing the border. I related it to my experiences patrolling along the Afghan/Pakistani border. The professor disagreed and despite what I viewed as an evidence-based, well-written paper, I received a less than stellar grade. After our conversation about the grade, it was obvious to me that if I had taken a different stance that he agreed with then I would have gotten a higher grade. Especially when I found out the girl next to me had written a paper that argued walls are immoral. If I could go back, I would have maybe written a different paper, I'd rather get a good grade than meaninglessly die on my sword. Make your own call, but like I said earlier, you need to play the game sometimes just like in the military. I had officers in the military suggest the dumbest things I've ever heard in Afghanistan, things that could get us all killed. I didn't say, "Sir, that's the dumbest fucking thing I've ever heard, you should never open your mouth again." I was, instead, respectful while suggesting a different course of action. Don't necessarily compromise who you are but make sure your future is more important to you than your ego.

Learning your professor and what they emphasize and care about will help your overall grade. What stance you want to take is entirely up to you. That's your decision, I'm just letting you know the reality. If you want to stand your ground with your personal beliefs, then go for it. If you are planning on writing papers that are adversarial to the professor's views, then you better write exceptional papers.

You will be able to tell the professors that care about politics immediately. Some teachers act as facilitators of discussion to get students talking and thinking, and some lecture you on their personal beliefs. I am not implying that all professors press down their political beliefs. You'll have professors that won't mention politics at all and some whose political ideologies dominate the classroom. You will see this in speakers that are invited to the college. At my school I never saw a conservative speaker, but I did see several democratic politicians, writers, and news personalities. Most student veterans tend to be somewhat conservative, and most professors are liberal. This combination can create clashes between student veterans and professors, especially those who are political advocates in their teaching or students that feel strongly about their beliefs. Your college classroom isn't the place to win hearts and minds. Your mission there is to learn, so focus on doing that. You can change the world after you get your degree. Don't let political distractions hurt your chances of completing your mission, which is graduating.

These views occasionally will spill over into anti-military comments or insensitive comments on current conflicts. I've seen veterans struggle with this, and I have myself. It can be difficult to sit quietly while professors bash the military and equally complicated to speak up. I probably spoke up confronting professors' inappropriate comments more than I should have, but not as much as I needed to. After all, my grade is what mattered to me, not what some professor thought of the military, wars, or current political affairs. Professors can be difficult to deal with when they treat their teaching secondary to their politics. However, part of college is learning how to effectively work with people who might disagree with you, that's going to be part of life outside of the military. The civilian world is more chaotic than what you are used to. In the military you have the sense everyone is on the same team. It doesn't feel that way in the civilian world.

Not everyone is on the line shooting in the same direction with a common goal, it's more adversarial.

In response to this, your military experience can offer an alternative opinion in the classroom. This greatly enriches the learning environment for everyone. Sometimes the problem in classrooms is a lack of diversity in thought, an echo chamber where the professor's politics are king and the students either don't care or are uninformed. The professor has spent years lecturing eighteen-year-olds in colleges, and veterans in the classroom change the dynamic. Good classes should intellectually challenge everyone, even the professor. The military is and has historically been an integral part of America. Your opinion, thoughts, and ideas matter. Your perspective in the class, based on your travels, training, inter-actions, and service, give you a small measure of authority in the classroom based on your military background. You have life experience, the other students do not or at least not to your level. The best professors are thrilled to have veterans in the room because they see the value of classroom diversity, but you aren't always going to have the best professors. Just make sure you are well-informed and be respectful. Feel free to speak up in the classroom about your beliefs, whatever they may be. But be warned, professors in college can pretty much grade you how they please, so tread carefully in your relationship with them.

You might not like your professor, you might even hate them, but go to class regardless. Your attendance in the class is important even if it's not counted toward your overall grade. You can't get full credit on a participation grade if you aren't there. It's beneficial to establish a positive class routine by being mentally and physically present in every class. Schedules and routines matter in college, just like in the military. Erratic routines in college will give you poor grades and bad experiences. You'll be far better off throughout college making an effort to establish positive relationships with your professors. Your actions should consistently demonstrate to them that you are making real effort, especially in classes you are struggling in. A solid question to ask all professors is what they recommend for extra help. They might provide you with other resources, offer extra credit, or explain things to you in more effective ways. Asking this question also demonstrates you care. If that doesn't work, then do your own research to supplement your in-class learning. YouTube videos are great for some people, especially visual learners. Whatever topic you are trying to learn or gain information about, there are five videos about it on YouTube. I guarantee it. YouTube has creative ways to explain things and there are many teachers that produce content on there. Don't solely rely on your professors, be willing to hunt for your own resources to help your learning.

You can also reach out to your classmates to form study groups, and you should especially do this before tests. It can be useful to study with other people, who might have different resources. Collaboration can be beneficial for everyone involved. In one of my psychology classes, a group of us would meet in the library before every quiz and review what was going to be on the quiz. Our group of students scored higher than the students that went at it solo. Form teams to help you succeed everywhere you go in college. Your library also has other sources, librarians are generally super helpful in assisting you. My college had a research librarian tucked away in the corner, and she helped me immensely by showing me research databases I didn't know existed. I did my senior thesis on suicide terrorism, and she found me primary resources of translated terrorist manifestos. Research is a skill that most student veterans don't bother to develop. There is more to effective research than the first page of a google search or Wikipedia. There are lots of underutilized academic resources you can take advantage of. I discovered the academic center at my college after a professor recommended it. They would edit and review my papers for me and catch things that I hadn't seen. This not only helped my grade but made me a better writer and a smarter person. You should work to use all the resources at your disposal to reach your potential success.

You can't get 100 percent on every assignment, sometimes you just have to work with what you've got and do your best. What you got might be a bad professor. You aren't alone. Some professors just ramble on and on about nothing and might slide one or two important pieces of information into the long lecture. I had professors that gave zero feedback on my work. I would hand in a paper and whether it said 100 or 70, there would be no information on it that I could use to make it better. I knew my work wasn't perfect, but it was frustrating to me since I didn't know how to improve. If you don't understand why you got a certain grade from your professor, you need to ask. Checking the syllabus can also provide useful information that a lot of people overlook. When you do get bad grades, advocate for yourself to the professor if you deem it necessary. Try to explain your reasoning, but don't argue for a higher grade without solid reasoning.

Unfair grades do happen in college. Make sure you approach the conversation with your professor about your grades nonthreateningly. Don't go in the discussion in crazy full veteran mode. I've seen people do that, and it never ends well. Be polite and try to avoid cursing too much. It can be a challenge to go from a military environment where cursing is the norm to academic environments where it is shocking and disrespectful to people. My first semester I would routinely curse in class discussions and not even notice it until a professor asked me to use more professional language. I asked another student about what the professor meant when he said "professional language," and he said that I said *fuck* sometimes. I was shocked. I didn't even realize I was cursing, it was just how I spoke after years in the military and in Afghanistan. The change in environment from the military to college means cursing in every sentence now is frowned upon. It's important to remember you are representing the military in your college as a student veteran. It might be hard, but don't tell people to fuck off, because civilians don't take it well, especially professors.

I do want to make it clear that I learned a lot from bad teachers, just like I learned a lot from bad leadership in the military. You learn what doesn't work for you, you learn how to be resilient, mature, and deal with shit. This is one of your strengths compared to your classmates since you've put up with far worse. I learned a lot in classes with bad professors because I had to do the legwork myself, where I had to put in extra hours to understand the material. Having bad teachers can make you more capable because you are going to have to deal with bad leadership in college and in the professional world. You can always control your attitude and your approach.

It is extremely useful to learn from those with opposing viewpoints and opinions, it forces you to reflect on your beliefs and reevaluate yourself. Taking the time to analyze other sides of arguments and even making opposing arguments yourself transforms you into a more educated, capable person. If you can learn how to argue effectively and noncombatively in college from either side of an issue, it will help you be successful in any future endeavors. In the military you can just say "Shut up" or "Roger that" and move on, but in college you are required to provide evidence and substantial research to support your opinions.

It does take two to tango, however. How you are approaching the class might need adjustment. Being a veteran, you might have a chip on your shoulder as well. You are responsible for your relationship to the professor and the class as well as your personal attitude. If you think your professor is wrong about advocating for socialism in the classroom or whatever they might be engaging in, turn in a well-written paper that shows evidence against that view. Or you can write the paper that they want and complain to your fellow student veterans to vent. Regardless, make the best decision for you and your goals. I was willing to swallow my pride for a better grade, and I saw other veterans unable to do that. My friend Doug, who is a combat veteran who served in Iraq and got hurt over there, couldn't deal very well with political professors. He would take offense when the professors bashed the wars overseas, and I get that, I really do, because it is tough when we have friends who have died there. He yelled at a professor because that specific professor called the deaths overseas worthless. He didn't feel like they were and deemed it hugely disrespectful to their memories.

You definitely don't want to get into a back-and-forth argument with the professor that isn't productive or educational. You're there to graduate college, not fight with your professor. A lot of veterans to this trap of arguing with professors in college and end up with a bad classroom experiences due to their aggressive approach. This leads to dropping classes and eventually dropping out. Especially if you are fresh out of the military, it can be hard to shake your mentality to survive the college classroom.

If there is such a thing as good teaching, then there is certainly such a thing as good learning. Be a good student and don't just assume the professor is responsible for your learning. You're the one responsible to learn it. A bad professor is no excuse for a bad grade, so you better find ways to figure that shit out. If you're really struggling that badly, it may be best to just drop the fucking class. You can take it another semester with a different professor instead of having a bad grade and a bad experience. Most of the time you can't do that, so just do your best. You can relax, doing poorly in one class or having one shitty teacher doesn't make or break your college experience. You'll probably have both scenarios during your college experience, but if you put in the effort, then the results will speak for themselves. The important thing is making it to the finish line of graduation, culminating in both developing your own academic potential and learning grit, including resilience to deal with less than perfect classroom situations. It's like your military contract when you were getting out, you can count down the days and when it's done, it's done. College degrees have immense value and anything of value has a cost that must be paid. A semester really isn't that long, and you don't have to see the professor every single day, so suck it up, buttercup.

The military is inflexible, but with college professors, everything is negotiable. Most professors are aware of the GI bill benefits and are cognizant of the fact that you must pass your class or may have to repay it. Negotiating for a better grade is always possible since college professors have freedom in their grading system. If you have a healthy relationship with your professor, then they will be more likely to hear you out and potentially raise your grade. Acting early is of primary importance. At the end of the semester professors are inundated with complaints, requests, and student problems. Don't be one of these problems, and act promptly if you have an issue with your grade. You should work on having an awareness of what your grade is before the professor submits it. One time I had a problem with a grade and it really stressed me out because I was concerned about my GPA for grad school. I was too stuck in a military mindset and didn't want to argue with the professor. I just said "Roger that" and moved on, which was definitely a mistake.

In the military, you get what you get when it comes to military schools. There isn't much wiggle room, and initially in college I just accepted the professor's grade even though I felt that it was unfair. It was not until my senior year that I was willing to advocate for myself with grades, and when I did it really helped me. I learned more in depth on how the professor graded, I got a deeper understanding of the material, and my grades were higher. I also learned valuable negotiating skills. When you go to your professor about your grade, make sure you have a solid case and some evidence on why they should review your grade. It is also worth just asking them if you can revise your work to get a higher grade.

When you do this, don't frame it as only caring about the grade, instead let the professor know you want a better understanding of the material. Sometimes grade adjustments are perfectly reasonable and the professor just mixed something up. If that isn't the case, make sure you go into your conversation with them well prepared. It is best to send an e-mail and ask to sit down to discuss your grade instead of just popping in. Don't ambush your professor or put them on the defensive. Discuss your thinking in a calm, reasonable way and use evidence in your conversation. It is best to be as specific as possible and refer to the syllabus or grading rubrics in your meeting.

When I started doing this in negotiating my grades, I tried to imagine it like I was asking for a raise. If you are asking for a raise, you should prove your point beyond a reasonable doubt if you want that boost. Don't complain or be a victim, but be honest. If you had some problems this semester, either personally or medically, then tell the professor that. Professors are people too, so if you have problems with your marriage, kids, work, the VA, or any other issues, then just let them know. Most professors understand veterans tend to be older, have more responsibilities, and comprehend the complexities of being a student veteran. It's not always going to work out, but if you do feel like you are being graded unfairly and the professor won't change the grade, then you can complain to the department head. I have never done that, but some of my friends have. I would only recommend doing this if you have a pretty strong case about your grade. Regardless, when you talk to the professor, be confident and stand up for your work.

If your relationship with your professor becomes unbearable, go speak with someone. I had an Army buddy in college who complained to the Dean that he was being discriminated against for being a veteran. He ended up getting a paper grade raised from a C- to an A. The professor had no rubric for grading the paper and graded papers that were significantly worse with a higher grade. The administration recognized that after their investigation. Most students would not have formally complained. My friend is kind of annoying and persistent, so it helped him out. Remember no one will advocate for you better than you. Colleges have rules that they cannot discriminate against people for veteran status, just like they can't discriminate based on race or gender. If you feel like this is the case, speak up to the professor, your adviser, or the administration. At the end of the semester, write an honest review about the professor to the school or online. You might save another veteran from a similar fate with a bad professor.

LEARN TO SAY NO

"Focus is about saying no."

Steve Jobs

Look at someone you respect, someone who is accomplished, rich, or famous. Chances are they have had to sometimes walk alone on their journey, taken chances and sacrificed weekends and holidays to accomplish their goals. Successful people put in the overtime required and acknowledge that anything of value comes with a cost. They have learned to say no to things that don't benefit them or align with their goals. I initially didn't say no. I met some guys in college, other veterans, and we would go out drinking. I didn't understand how I only had one enemy in life, and it was me. Maybe the Taliban, but they don't count in this situation. I was engaging in self-defeating behaviors, and it was expensive and draining. I would go out and get drunk on school nights and suffer during my morning classes. I wouldn't be mentally present or as sharp as I needed to be. I wouldn't do the assigned readings before class because I'd be at a bar or recovering from the bar. I had lost part of my ambition and drive after the military. My grades declined, my health deteriorated, and my attitude sucked. I was sabotaging my own life, my own future, and for what? Just some meaningless fun that had no long-term benefit. I had to give up some short-time thrills and happiness to achieve the success I wanted. I realized everyone has a hard road in life, especially veterans, and I was making my road in life harder to travel down.

You need to ask yourself and those around you what things you might be doing to sabotage your own life. Just like me, you are your own worst enemy and only you can stop you. I didn't fully realize what I was doing to myself. I was holding myself back from my full potential. I was bowing down to unproductivity. The worst thing about it was, after I figured it out, I kept doing it. I was taking the easy road, it was going to be hard to stay home and study and say no to a good time. My first semester I was doing what was fun and easy, which was going to give me a hard life in the future because of consistent poor decisions. Eventually I realized I needed to do what was hard now so I could have an easier life later. I was screwing over my future self. If I failed out of college, and this would be my third time failing out, my life was going be painful. I would have to live with myself, a combat veteran with PTSD who failed out of college three times. Not exactly a winner or someone you would want to hire. I was going to be a prisoner to this failing mentality forever. If I failed again, I might not survive it.

I had to ask myself some serious questions when my grades started slipping. It's difficult to be brutally honest with yourself. It was tough for me to look in the mirror and ask and answer the hard questions of life and who I wanted to be. It's easy to see obvious problems in your friends or family, but seeing them in yourself is more complicated. Many of the guys I was hanging out with weren't in school, they were working and partying and that was about it. I didn't want any of their lives, but for some reason I was hanging around them. I read a quote that said, "If you hang out with four losers, you'll be the fifth." These guys weren't necessarily losers, but they weren't ever going to be rich or change the world either. I didn't have a backup plan getting out of the military, I was going to go to college and if that didn't work for me, I had no clue what to do. In order to stop my own self-sabotage, I had to negotiate with the enemy within.

I figured out I wasn't in the situation that I wanted to be in, but I wasn't sure how to break out of it. I wasn't sure how to say no, the Army taught me to say "Roger that." I couldn't improve my life unless I changed my behavior, then stuck to it. I found it was easy to break promises to myself, I told myself I wasn't going to go out on Thursday because I had class Friday morning. But Thursday night football was on and everyone was going out, so there I went. I had to figure out how to keep the promises I made to myself, so I specified my goals. If you have vague goals, like you are going to do well in school, then it's easy to fail. Make your goals as specific as you possibly can. I was going to get straight As. As a veteran you are so used to this rigid military structure and then when it vanishes, you sort of wander around, looking for purpose. If you don't know where you are going than you will never get there. I set up a schedule, and you should create your own schedule that works for you.

I changed my life so I wouldn't touch alcohol except on weekends, and soon this transformed to only drinking on Saturdays. No matter what. I would only drink four times a month and kept to it during the semester. I negotiated with myself like I wanted to help myself. I asked myself if I came to me for advice, what would I say? I communicated with my mentor, who didn't even drink except on special occasions. She would either work in the evening or study. Now she's got a great corporate gig and has been steadily getting promoted on her way up the corporate chain. She learned to say no and told me that if I'm not going to care about something a year from now, then don't care about it that weekend. I knew I wasn't going to care about a random Saturday night out in a year, but I would care about my economics grade.

Her ability to say no made her successful. She asked me what I was out celebrating anyway? I have no idea what I was celebrating, but I was out partying like I had won the Superbowl. It's entirely possible you are out celebrating like that too. The more I celebrated, the less happy I was. I wasn't celebrating anything worthwhile, there was no accomplishment, no victory and no triumph. When I stopped partying, I started finding reasons to stay home. Soon I started doing better in school and in life. I started setting my days up with purpose and scheduling them to be productive days. I wanted to be in better shape toward the future I wanted than when I started that day. I had more money in the bank and had more time to be productive when I started scheduling my days to meet my goals. I was going to make a difference, be successful, and make the world a better place, as opposed to being drunk at a bar telling war stories.

There's nothing wrong with being a drunk idiot at bars occasionally, but this is best done in moderation, not every weekend. Military awards and medals aren't given for potential, and grades aren't given for your potential either. They reflect the effort that you put in. When I stopped partying my wallet was fatter, my body was healthier, and I wasn't drunk texting people I shouldn't have. I started getting a little stronger and smarter each day when I stopped drinking so much. I recommend you have a good time at college but not such a good time it interferes with your future self. Same with smoking weed or other vices, say no when you need to. Wake up determined and go to bed satisfied with your day, each day inching closer to your goal of graduation.

In all likelihood, you probably felt how I felt starting college: behind. It was hard to not draw comparisons between my myself and the other students. Even if you only did one enlistment and are starting college in your early twenties after getting out, you'll feel similar. I felt so far behind in life, sitting in freshmen college classes at thirty. Veterans commonly feel out of place. I got wrapped up in the comparisons and it's easy for you to do the same. It's a trap many veterans fall into and is difficult to escape from. Work to reframe your thought process. To do this, it is necessary to compare yourself to who you were yesterday, not to who other people are today. To do this, you can put a mirror next to your bed. When you get into bed at night, compare yourself to the person you saw that morning. Is that person further or closer to your goals, is that person healthier or unhealthier, is that person richer or poorer than who you saw that morning?

Instead of looking at the kid next to you and wanting to strangle them, look at yourself. When you look at yourself, think of all the amazing things you have accomplished, the places you've traveled, and the training you've had. Reflect on your past experiences, you know yourself and your past and you don't know the other students. You can get better each day.

The other students didn't step up during a time of war and serve their country; you did. Be proud of that. Instead of comparing yourself to other students, compare yourself to who you were yesterday, last week, or even last month. You aren't going to be a totally different person week to week, but if you are just slightly superior to the person you were last week, then you are moving in the right damn direction. If you are slightly inferior to who you were last week, or further from your goals, then it is appropriate to reflect, speak with your mentor, and figure out how to reverse course. If you keep this up every week for a year, then you'll find yourself in a much better place. You have to say no to making social comparisons to your classmates.

The second comparison trap you might be likely to fall into is you versus your friends. When I started college at thirty years old, all my high school friends had graduated college ten years earlier, or they didn't go. They were mostly set in their careers, well established in their communities, and had kids. You might have kids too or a spouse but are less established in life due to transitioning out of the military. We move around a lot, so it can be tough to establish roots. I felt like everyone else was already running the race of life and I wasn't even at the starting line despite being thirty years old. I was comparing myself to them. What I eventually realized is that they were not running the same race that I was running. My goals were not my friends' goals. I was stuck in a negative self-loop. Breaking out of that mindset gave me freedom.

You are running a race against the you that existed yesterday, and you need to run hard every day in college. To do this, you need to set your own standards of performance to get where you want to go, not meet other people's expectations of you. The people you think are judging you for starting college late have their own problems. You aren't going to win or succeed by trying to be them or settling in a job that doesn't challenge you. If you are focused on comparing yourself to others, you'll never actualize your full potential. You need to be proud to be different, be proud to be a veteran who answered the call to service when others refused. You should stand tall and say no to comparing yourself to your friends and classmates, even who they pretend to be online.

You should be saying no to partying if you are getting C's. The military doesn't celebrate mediocrity, and neither should you. If you crush a test, meet a life goal, or do something amazing, then go celebrate that. If you are getting average grades or, worse, failing, you need to reevaluate your priorities. Take care of your responsibilities like your marriage, work, and kids, but evaluate where you are wasting time. We all waste time. I had veterans in my student veteran club stay up every night playing video games. It's obvious that thirty hours of Xbox per week isn't going to accomplish much. I wasn't where I wanted to be in school or life, and yet I was out partying every weekend my first semester. Say no to social media, no to Netflix binge-watching, no to the bar, and yes to the library if you're sucking in college.

If you are trying to write a paper or study for a test, you shouldn't have your favorite TV show on in the background. I'll tell you from experience and backed up by research, multi-screen studying is inefficient and doesn't work. Say no to that. If you are watching TV shows, listening to music, and texting while studying it just isn't going to be productive. Your friends are not going to be very good study partners unless you're all focused. I tried studying with two infantry buddies at school, it never worked out. We would end up talking about deployments, girls, or anything other than concentrating on our material. One time the three of us sat down to study and promptly decided we should go to the bar and have a beer.

What could you accomplish if you gave all of yourself to your future, said no to every fun activity, and instead spent every weekend studying? One weekend during my second semester at college we had a four-day weekend. Some of my buddies were going partying, taking a trip somewhere, or just celebrating having a long weekend. Usually, I'm all in on having a good time, but this weekend I tried something different and surprised myself. I had a bunch of house chores and errands I had been putting off as well as some schoolwork to get done and one paper I had coming down to the wire. I told myself I wasn't going to go out at all this weekend, wasn't going to hang out with any girls, I was just going to get shit done. I couldn't believe the results at the end of the long weekend when I was focused for only four short days. I absolutely killed the morning when usually I would be recovering from the night before. I also was able to make myself breakfast and woke up ready to take on the day. The whole weekend went like that. I managed to not only get one paper done but two and worked ahead on other homework assignments. I cleaned my entire house, did every chore that I'd put off for a month, and worked out every day. At the end of the weekend I was so impressed with myself I realized I had been wasting my weekends before. When I started winning the morning, then I began winning the day. Honestly, I don't understand how people who don't drink don't just take over the world. The rest of us are too busy partying or recovering to notice, especially since gone were the days when I was twenty and could drink all night and get up and run ten miles. I realized I was bullshitting myself before. I thought I had been working hard at college, but I hadn't been. If I continued partying things were going to get worse.

You can always make it worse. What I mean by this is that when things start going downhill, you get a bad grade, have a bad day or whatever else goes wrong, you can always make it worse. Don't be overly fixated on every grade so much it stresses you out, but take your grades seriously. Think of the worst field op you have been on, then it starts raining. The military can always make things worse, you know that. If you get a bad grade on a paper or a test, that class is going to get worse if you don't get your shit together. A weak mind will take a bad class, grade, or experience and ruin the rest of the semester. Don't get a bad grade and go out drinking, get a bad grade and go to the library. If you get that first bad grade and don't take action to correct it and learn from your mistakes, it's going to spiral down from there. Using a resilient veteran mindset, your one bad grade, class, or experience should motivate you to say no to whatever you were doing that caused it.

It is easy to be distracted as a student veteran because you have more going on than the other students. You might have a family, bills, PTSD, mortgage, responsibilities, VA appointments, and more preoccupations other students don't have. Because of this you need to say no to every unimportant distraction that will damage your college learning and experience. You must learn to say no.

BUILD YOUR ARMOR

"As long as you brothers support one another and render assistance to one another, your enemies can never gain victory over you. But if you fall away from each other your enemy can break you like frail arrows, one at a time."

Genghis Khan

It's difficult to gain real college success totally solo without support. I've seen these types of veterans at my college, they don't want to interact with the rest of the veteran population at the school or be involved in school activities, clubs, or groups. You'll be a more effective student and well-adjusted person if you can build support systems for yourself, like armor. Everyone gets out of the military for their own personal reasons and I understand the feeling of not wanting to feel like you're still in by surrounding yourself with veterans. While you are serving you are a member of the greatest team on earth. The number one thing most veterans say they miss when they get out is the camaraderie and brother/sisterhood. To combat this, most modern institutions have student veteran groups on campus. SVA (Student Veterans of America) group at my school provided an exceptional support system for me. My membership allowed me to stay involved in the veteran community, volunteer, make friends, and be around like-minded individuals. The SVA was officially created nationally in 2008 to deal with the unique needs of OEF/OIF veterans returning home from conflict zones.

My school did an amazing job at supporting veterans. We had our own Veteran Resource Center, which was a room that was exclusively for veteran use. It had a fridge, TV, coffee, and computers we could use. We could hang out in there and watch Jocko, Shapiro, or Joe Rogan podcasts, war movies, or whatever else while hanging with fellow student veterans. We could have student veteran meetings and have veteran-centered events in there. At the risk of embarrassing myself by saying this, it was a "veteran safe space." In addition, we had a veteran service officer who worked for the school, but her job was to help the veteran population with whatever we might need. It removed some of the isolation we felt in the college world. I pretty much lived in that room during my time at college, we could decorate the room at holidays and just hang out in a military-friendly environment between classes and bullshit around. I'm not sure whether the school gave us the room so all the student veterans with tattoos who cursed a lot wouldn't bother the rest of the students or out of genuine assistance for student veterans, but it doesn't matter. Veteran dropout rates, suicide rates, homelessness rates, and other problems are high because of the loss of community after getting out of the military. Student veteran organizations at your campus can give you back that community and return the sense of camaraderie you miss. It did for me, and I met some great friends and amazing people who were like me. They were trying to better their lives after military service through education.

Such considerable isolation that can occur for student veterans. I was ten years older than everyone in pretty much all my classes, and it was difficult. I couldn't relate to them and they definitely couldn't relate to me. The SVA helped me feel engaged in student life and like an actual college student. We did activities on campus and had a military ball every year on Veterans Day. We also had the opportunity to educate other students on military life and our experiences. It was a military-friendly school, and I desperately needed that. However, not all schools are so friendly or welcoming to veterans, I promise. You should look for a college environment that has support systems in place for student veterans or that advertises strong veteran programs. Veterans understand one another, much more than your local friends or classmates will, and this helped me feel part of a team again by being active in my SVA and my college.

Some veterans aren't sure if they want to be part of the SVA at their school or what role their military service should play in education. I knew my first day that I didn't necessarily want to be singled out as different from the other students, but I also didn't want to just be lumped in with the rest of the eighteen-year-old students in the classroom. The student veteran groups can also help you answer any questions you have about your benefits or specific GI Bill questions. When you pick a military-friendly college you can face the college challenge as part of a veteran team and not a solitary individual. This team will have similar backgrounds and shared experiences that make forging friendships easy, whereas you might struggle with making BFF's with traditional students.

The college you pick is more important than you might think. I know I didn't want to sit in 300-seat lecture halls. I wanted to be around other veterans and have discussions. Some schools may not have a military-friendly environment or student culture that is positive towards veterans. You need people who have your back in your school, we would help each other out and look out for one another, just like in the military. It is going to be challenging for you at times to connect with non-veteran students, it sure was for me. Being an active member in your student veteran group at school will combat feelings of isolation and provide an opportunity to gain like-minded teammates and friends.

The camaraderie is something that you will miss if you choose to do only online classes. If you are anything like most veterans, you need that camaraderie. Go ahead and do what works for you, but I prefer hands-on, experiential learning, which is difficult to get online. I learn much more in person than online as I think most people tend to do, especially veterans. Online school always seemed stupid and noneducational to me but do what works for you. You are also learning valuable communication and interpersonal skills during in-class instruction, like learning how to deal with civilians. The military mindset will help you, but you do have to recognize you aren't in the military anymore. It's time to learn how to deal with the world again. I would recommend taking your classes in person whenever possible. While you're in this environment, you don't need to only deal with fellow veterans. Investigate other student groups as well. You can join a fraternity or sorority and get to know civilians; you are one now, after all. Embrace your veteran identity but don't forget to be a normal person sometimes. There are a lot of good opportunities on campus outside of merely veteran activities.

There are so many more potential veteran groups in your area that you can be a member of now that you are out. Don't ignore them. I happened to be in an area with a high concentration of veterans, and I joined four veteran groups. Younger veterans are tending to avoid the classic veteran service organizations like the Veterans of Foreign Wars and the American Legion. I joined both. These two groups have held the line and fought for veteran benefits and our rights in Washington, D.C. They are more established and have more political sway and power, which can potentially help you with employment in the future. As the next generation of veterans, we need to keep alive these groups that fight on our behalf for the sake of future veterans. With the power of these groups also comes money and resources. They also have funds that can help you out if you hit a rough spot. If you are a full-time student veteran and your car breaks down, these groups will help you. I've seen them do exactly that for student veterans at my school—pay a month's rent, help around the holidays, and pay to fix a broke-down vehicle. The VFW also helped pay childcare expenses for a single parent veteran that I know so she could attend her classes. You can also apply for scholarships through these bigger organizations, as well as education help and legal advice. There are a wide range of benefits to joining these organizations. And beer is usually cheap there, so that's a plus.

One of the other groups I joined was a fitness organization that helped veterans called the Airborne Tri Team. One of the things veterans lose when they get out is their physical fitness, let's face it when you aren't being forced to run every morning you might get fat. For some people, the military ruins working out because it's part of your job, so that's the first thing to go when you get out. I don't really need to tell you this, but exercise is good for you and for your brain, which is important in college. I have had a tremendous time with this small organization in being a part of a team and making lifelong friends. Our mission is to provide war veterans with opportunities and goal-oriented physical achievements to maximize veteran potential, and to build self-esteem by being part of a team. As a team, we would participate in 5K's, obstacle course races, triathlons, bike rides and more. We would bring veterans together and give them physical challenges and undertake them ourselves as part of a team. The VA's answer to a lot of the mental and physical problems veterans face is to give them pills. We, on the other hand, gave them fitness and friendship. At the end of all our races, we do twenty-two pushups representing the twenty-two veterans that take their lives each day in order to bring awareness to veteran suicide and mental health issues. I think fitness is important for veterans when they get out and something people tend to overlook in their college experience. You don't want to be the old veteran who can't even get into their uniform because you turned into such a fat ass. If you work out regularly, it will help you have more energy, feel better, and be a better student. Simply put, people that work out tend to have happier lives and not be as depressed as people that don't. An unhealthy lifestyle will harm your educational and personal goals. Don't abandon the warrior mentality because you're a civilian now. Continue to train your mind and body in college.

If you get involved in groups like this, then you'll be a healthier college student, and healthier college students tend to perform better academically. You also can give back to your community using your military experience. We would go work out with Boy Scouts and deliver toys to kids around Christmas to represent the military in a positive way. Connecting with others in this way will help you be more socially, emotionally, and physically healthy and better equipped to tackle your college classes.

The other group I belonged to that helped me out, was my motorcycle club. My motorcycle club helped me deal with my PTSD and find friends to ride with while also reinforcing my military mindset. I started off as a prospect in the US Military Vets Motorcycle Club and loved the camaraderie and brotherhood. To deal with my issues that stemmed from military service, I rode motorcycles. On a motorcycle you're focused on what you are doing, and it is a therapeutic experience. It helped me deal with my PTSD and the stress of school. I was also able to give back to my community, participate in military events, and do a lot of charity work with my club. You should put energy into searching for your own personal ways to escape stress.

I'm not advocating you go out tomorrow and buy a motorcycle, but I would encourage you to find unique ways to deal with your stress to be successful in college. Find your own supportive communities. While you're in college, you need to work to be successful outside of school to be successful in school. There are great organizations in your community. A buddy of mine got really into a program for horseback riding for veterans, which was effective for him. I have another friend who participated in veteran art classes to deal with his PTSD and another still who did stand-up comedy. Go do yoga or something. The point I'm making is, if you want to be successful in the classroom, then you have to be successful outside the classroom as well.

Unlike in the military though, my support networks when I got out didn't just appear in front of me. Instead I had to build my support system from the ground up around myself like armor. It took time and effort to make the relationships and connect with others. Connecting with others allows you to become, once again, a part of something greater than yourself. This will be instrumental in personal success and happiness while diminishing potential problems that veterans frequently encounter.

In these organizations, you get to make an impact on the world and yourself. Your membership in them will give you the tools, resources, and connections you need to be successful in college and beyond. We learned a lot about teamwork in the military and now it's time to build your own team to help you be successful in the real world. You never went at anything in the military alone, don't do it in college either. Build your armor.

LIGHTEN YOUR LOAD

"Somewhere inside, we hear a voice. It leads us in the direction of the person we wish to become. But it is up to us whether or not to follow."

Pat Tillman

The military teaches you many different things, arguably the most important being perseverance. It is ingrained in the heart of all veterans to "embrace the suck" and meet any and all challenges head on. So it is no surprise that when veterans enter the college world, they sometimes take on just a little too much. To the point where they must tread water barely keeping their head above the surface, or, worst-case scenario, they end up drowning. When I was deployed before long dismounted patrols, I would look for any ways I could to lighten my load. When you're exhausted, fifty pounds feels a lot lighter than seventy on your back.

I watched veteran after veteran just take on too much,

including myself. When starting college, it's best not to approach it the same way you would beginning something new in the military. There are challenges that college will bring that the military just didn't. In the military you had backup for every mission, and that doesn't exist at school. Yes, you have been able to survive what you might deem "harder" things during your time in the military. But college will present you with a unique set of new challenges to grapple with. Not to mention the difficulty of transitioning to a whole new way of life, the mysterious civilian world. Give yourself a chance to get a lay of the land before you dive into the deep end head first. By that I mean, don't overdo it, especially not your first semester.

I've seen plenty of veterans run themselves into the ground taking more credits than necessary and working full time while attending class full time. They split their focus into too many areas rather than devoting enough attention to their primary goals. They just spread themselves too thin, which is easy to do. These veterans either drop out and are never seen again or have low grades or are overwhelmed and stressed throughout college. It's easier to do than you might think. Sometimes extenuating circumstances can present themselves and throw a wrench into your plans; life happens. While this can happen to any student, we veterans are more likely to experience unique circumstances that can pull our attention from our studies. You might encounter marital, money, health, or childcare issues that other students are less likely to encounter. The veteran dropout rates remain high because college can overwhelm you during an already stressful transition to civilian life. You are used to structure, leadership, and a very specific way of life. It is normal to be stressed about what life outside of the military will be like, and college is a great first step to a successful future. If you are dedicated to your education, you must commit to making your degree your primary focus and lighten your load when you can. Rather than just "getting your degree," you must make the decision to be as successful as possible, and to put your studies first when you need to. In order to ensure your success, it is imperative to only take on what you can absolutely handle. If you need to work while in college, try to take a job that does not require as much mental energy, or even an on-campus job that will allow you to study while working. If you know you will have family obligations, make sure you schedule your classes and study time so that you are meeting your obligations, but also not letting your schoolwork slip. It is possible to be a successful student while working, taking care of a family or managing any number of other responsibilities. In order to do so, you will have to manage your time wisely, and prioritize efficiently.

One veteran I met was named Sam. Sam was only taking four classes (twelve credits, which is full-time) but also worked part time and had kids. It only took Sam a few weeks to get behind and start falling apart trying to manage his hectic life. Sam said he didn't realize all the work he would have to do outside of class, and it was hard to get work done when he was with his kids, and his job was stressful and time-consuming. Very quickly he started sleeping poorly (as you may know veterans already have trouble sleeping), he was eating unhealthy food, and he was finding it difficult to get to his VA therapy appointments around his school schedule. Energy is finite. Nobody is the energizer bunny, and Sam slowly disintegrated under the weight of trying to maintain all his priorities. His load was too much and his marriage suffered, he started failing classes and he was never able to find time to recharge himself. I called him when I hadn't seen him in a few days, to find that he was staying home that week with a sick child and was unable to come to class. I offered to come watch his kids for him while he went to class but he refused. I offered to go talk to his professor for him, but he refused. I offered to record his class for him, but he refused. Not long after, he dropped out. I never saw him at school again. Sam's load was too heavy for him to carry.

Life problems and issues are going to arise while you're at college, it is inevitable. You simply need to practice good time management, prioritize, and remember that you aren't Captain America. Don't forget to rest and lighten your load when you can.

I faced my own challenges with starting college. I was unrealistic about how much time I had and how much time I needed to dedicate to my studies, work, and life. I too was biting off more than I could chew and didn't even know it. I was trying to do my best with work, school, family and life. I was constantly struggling to understand how much time it would take me to do a task. I thought I could write papers the day before they were due and that like in the military, I would work best under pressure. This was shortsighted. I ended up turning in half-ass work that I didn't get a chance to review, let alone let someone else give me their input. Plus, the professors could tell that I was procrastinating as I was submitting work that was due at midnight at 11:55 p.m. in most cases. Working under time pressure gave me anxiety and made me feel constantly behind. I didn't turn in quality work or learn anything from doing the assignments. It is important to realize that you aren't just there to submit the work and get a grade. You're in college to learn, and if you are rushing work and not putting the required effort in, you're missing out on the learning. In college you are also developing important skills such as reading, writing and analytical thinking. You don't rush successful operations in the military, and you shouldn't rush your college assignments.

Taking a conscious effort to lighten your load will strengthen your ability to take on your challenges. You must be realistic with yourself when you are preparing for school. Kind of like a new year's resolution, we all know that person that promises each year to lose 100 pounds then proceeds to lose zero. They are biting off more than they can realistically chew. If they say they want to lose twenty pounds, that seems more doable. If the odds against you seem insurmountable it can be easier to justify quitting or failing against impossible odds. By starting slow, you allow yourself time to adjust, you will have a chance to get your feet under you and learn what works and what doesn't. Then you can shoulder a heavier burden. Take the minimum amount of credits to be a full-time student, especially in the first semester. The problem with taking on more than you can carry is that in college it can be tough to catch up once you start slipping behind. The assignments and work will only continue to pile up and eventually, you'll collapse under their weight.

In a perfect world, you won't have to work while going to college, but chances are you will. I knew a female student veteran who loved her job as a gymnastics coach and could never see how much the job was draining her and distracting her from her already heavy course load. She was taking eighteen credits during the day and driving over an hour each way to coach gymnastics until 9 p.m. every night and traveling every weekend for competitions. She was so invested in the kids she was coaching that it was hard to focus on school. She would try to fit in school assignments in the small breaks she got if she got to work early or if there was a break in the competitions. As you can imagine, this was extremely hard to sustain and though she was smart and capable of getting great grades, she squeaked by. While that is by no means failure, she constantly felt behind and would proclaim that she was a "walking ball of stress." Though she was doing well juggling her job and school, can you imagine what she could have done with even a slightly less demanding job? While sometimes you might have to take a job based on financial need, it's important to at least communicate to the job that school is of primary importance to you and that you might require some flexibility. Being able to take time off around midterms or finals is important and can help keep your stress levels down. The fact that your minimum-wage job became too demanding is a pretty dumb reason to quit school.

It's an innate desire to want to sprint to the finish line

of college and graduate as quickly as possible. If you run too hard you could pull a muscle, which could delay your completion or, worst case, take you out of the race completely. It is important to know the warning signs, and how to mitigate failure before it happens. Just like in the military, look for points in a mission where things could go wrong and create contingencies and backups. Some of the first warning signs is if you are tired all the time (sound familiar?), you aren't sleeping, and your body aches. That's an indicator you might need to find ways to lighten your load. Other indicators can be if you are struggling to pay attention and can't retain new information effectively. It is hard to write papers or pass tests when you're struggling to retain the information that is being taught to you. When you start to feel like this, it is imperative that you ask for help. Before your problems become insurmountable. Take a mental health day if you need it, you can't do it in the military but the civilian world is a little more relaxed.

The great thing about college is it is set up to help you succeed, there are free tutoring labs, resources, and study groups. It is important to remember that your professors are human too. They will respect your honesty and will be more likely to work with you if you address your struggles before they become catastrophic failures.

Once I recognized that I was struggling, I started applying military reasoning to my assignments. I started assignments early, often as soon as they were assigned, so that I wasn't rushed. Often, professors offered the option to turn the work in a week ahead so they could give you critiques, and by the time I resubmitted it, it was much better. It wasn't necessarily because I was brilliant but instead because I was planning with the end goal in mind, which was to get an A. Additionally, reviewing and rewriting the papers multiple times entrenched the information in my mind, which then allowed me to do better on the exams. I found it easier to manage my schedule when I was compartmentalizing. School, life, and other aspects of being a veteran can pull you in a bunch of different directions, and you'll have to make a conscious effort to focus on one thing at a time. Deal with one assignment, project, or class at a time instead of trying to do a bunch of things at once. Effectively prioritizing your classwork is what is going to make or break you as a student.

You have more freedoms in college, and with this freedom comes more opportunities to screw it up. If you take on too much, you're going to fall behind before you even have a chance to start. Stress is a killer for veterans in college who are likely already facing enormous pressure. Stress was ruining my ability to learn and retain information. Even if I knew the material, when I was overstressed my schoolwork suffered. My brain just wasn't working the way I wanted it to when I got too stressed. I thought if I studied more then I would get better grades, turned out that isn't always the case. I burned myself out. It isn't about the hours spent studying but the efficiency of your studying. Instead of studying while watching *The Office* on Netflix, I would listen to some classical music on my headphones in a corner of the library. It is going to take some time and experimentation to figure out your sweet spot for studying. Find a place where you can quietly focus and get locked in to studying.

You might as well expect to be overwhelmed at some point during college. If you aren't then you probably aren't putting the effort in or challenging yourself. Anticipating the potential problems can help you prepare for it. Accept that a certain amount of stress is inevitable and even healthy. A final should stress you a bit because it's important. To deal with it, take some mental breaks, relax a bit by finding ways to relieve your stress, and talk to your mentor or fellow veterans. Some things can't be changed, and stress in college is one of them, so you might as well embrace it, prepare for it and kick ass. While you can't predict what life will bring during your college career, you can make every effort to drop the things that don't matter and lighten your load.

AFTER ACTION REVIEW

"A warrior must only take care that his spirit is never broken".

Shissai

College is hard, harder still if you are your own enemy. If you eliminate the enemy within, you can take on all the outside challenges in the world. I really struggled mentally in college, trying to figure out who the hell I was after the military. The military defines us for a while when we get out. It always takes longer to adjust than you think it will. I knew I wanted to be successful, and I'm sure you want that for yourself. I didn't want to be one of the twenty-two, or another disgruntled veteran at a bar reliving war stories. There had to be a way to transmit my military skills into academic success in college. It took me a while to figure it out but when I was working to help others, I was improving myself. When I treated college like my military contract, I discovered what true commitment could produce. I was able to see how my years in the military could be used to help and not hurt me in college. I sat in front, and I embraced my veteran grit. I searched out people to mentor me and for me to mentor. I built up my armor and I lightened my load. Importantly for me, I learned how to say no when I needed to. I hope you learned something from this book and can move forward or continue your college career and life with purpose and success. I would appreciate you passing the information along, paying it forward to other veterans. We are a team, working for the betterment of our nation, and your time making the world a better and safer place shouldn't stop when you take off the uniform. Good luck.

I would love to hear about your college experiences and stories. If you enjoyed the book, consider leaving a review on Amazon. For any questions or comments, I can be reached at:

Combat2CollegeBook@gmail.com
Facebook.com/john.h.davis.writer

Thank you for your service,

John H Davis
Staff Sergeant, US Army

CPSIA information can be obtained
at www.ICGtesting.com
Printed in the USA
BVHW051315290722
643329BV00006B/513

9 780578 663388